An Angel's Journey

A   Story

By

Angela M Grout

ISBN# 9781507544754
LSSN- TX0007242120/2009-06-30

Cover artwork: Create Space
Editor: Patricia Fry

Unless otherwise indicated, all writings are by the author.

For Additional Information, please contact:
Angela Grout
430 Main St
Agawam, MA 01001
413-786-7427

Printed in the USA
CreateSpace
7290 Investment Drive, Suite B; North Charlestown, SC 29418

Reason is the human tool by which we try to know and understand the world. Revelation is a divine gift which we must humbly receive.

~Saint Thomas Aquinas

For

Maggie & Molly

March 1999

I awake and hear the voice so much stronger than before. My tears are flowing as if cleansing my soul.

I'd just had the deepest sleep I can remember. I was dreaming about a shower, a beautiful shower with sunrays beaming, rainbows shining, and angelic music playing. I enjoyed a conversation with St. Theresa as the echo of angels sang, 'Make me a channel of your peace, where there is injury, your pardon Lord; and where there's doubt, true faith in you.'

Again, I have had a visit with an angel, and this time I get to share it. Over nine hours shall pass to tell this angel's journey.

1-2-3 Let's go...

1

Arriving Home

Every end turns into Something New...

Let the journey continue.

Today, I died. It was a death I knew was coming. I considered myself spiritual and mentally prepared, yet I was unaware of how quickly the transition to an afterlife could happen.

I was thirty-one years old and didn't understand why my life had to end so soon. I was preparing for a future. Why wasn't I getting one? Would I still have a future in an afterlife?

I had many questions. My family taught me about heaven as a child, but other than merely a place where you go when you die, I didn't know much about it. Toward the end of my life, I often asked questions about heaven, but no one would discuss it with me. My mother would tell me not to worry about heaven because, as far as she was concerned, I wasn't going anywhere.

I tried to talk with her about my impending death, but she denied that I was even dying. I had to believe that if there was a God, I would find my answers with him and in this place called heaven. I was hopeful that I would discover a way to tell my mother I was okay if I did make it to heaven.

My name is Rhealynn, and this is the story of my journey home.

Moments before I passed over and I was still in my physical body, I was able to hold my mother's hand. As weak as I was, I held on tight trying to send messages of love to her and to my entire family. They kept asking me if I was okay. "I am okay," I say, "I am okay," but they could not hear me. My voice was no longer audible to them.

My mother cries as I take my last breath. I place my hand on her shoulder, squeezing it, then realize it is not my physical hand that is touching her, it is my spirit. She puts her hand on her shoulder, thinking she felt my hand, but then dismisses the thought.

Oh my, I just realized that I made it. I have survived death. I have made the crossover to an afterlife. How instant that was. How painless. How incredibly awesome, I still feel part of the world, but somehow not physically. My goal at this moment is to find a way to assure my family that I am perfectly okay. I survived death. Wow...I am in awe. I am more than okay, I am with God.

Images of my life are presented to me. I'm shown all the good things I accomplished and every life that I had touched. Unconditional love encircles me as a party of angels, and the most wonderful sound trumpets can make invite me into the most radiant lights. An extreme healing energy embraces my soul.

Family members, have arrived before me and welcome me back. We all merge into one in this incredible comforting energy. I am in the center of the most beautiful and peaceful place ever. It feels and looks like a garden, but so much more.

The fragrance of gardenias dance around us as I am embraced by God. He embraces my spirit and I truly become one with Him. There is no adjective to describe Him, except unconditionally powerful, loving, and omniscient. He communicates with actions of love. He talks with me, but to describe the words he uses, I cannot. All I can say is wait…when you meet Him, you will know.

As we embrace, my earthly questions flow. Why did I have such a short life? Why did my mother and family have to suffer over my death? Why, why, why? So many questions pour out of my soul, and they are all answered with complete clarity.

I discover that I have infinite wisdom. I know that I have always been here, but during my earthly life, I was denied the knowledge of remembering the details of this place. I am where I need to be now and my soul is rediscovering its home.

As I questioned why I was taken from my earthly life, I heard this answer; "Rhealynn, don't confuse your physical life with your spiritual life. The two are not separate, but mere parts of each other. All life is eternal for this reason." With that explanation, I saw the plan.

I want to describe the plan to you, but there are no words to translate it. However, I can tell you, that it is a masterpiece. What a blessing to see this big picture; yet there is a catch once you cross over. I am allowed to see everything. Not only can I see everyone I love at all times, I also know what is going to happen to them. Even with this knowledge, I cannot prevent anything from happening to them. I know I am going to struggle with this.

Watching people suffer is hard; especially now, since I know the end result of what God has intended and they cannot see that beauty. Even if you have the faith to move mountains, no one except God has the power to change the plan.

God reveals to me that when something wonderful happens, it will be beautiful to watch, like a sunrise. But when something terrible has to happen, it will be uncomfortable to witness without wanting to fix it. I remember when mom was diagnosed with breast cancer; watching her struggle through chemo was unbearable and there wasn't much I could do. When the treatment was over, we both knew it was worth the battle. So she lost her hair, her eyebrows, a lot of weight and even her pride during the battle, but she didn't lose her life. And I didn't lose my mom.

You might be wondering why she had to lose her daughter, and I am telling this story to share that she didn't. I am with her always. Yes, I lost my physical life but the love a mother has for her child never ends, which is why I survived.

Sometimes a miracle arrives to heal you physically and other times a miracle arrives to heal you spiritually. God knows what you need and he does provide. Trust that everything is for the best because He alone knows how to finish for perfection. And his masterpiece is perfection.

2

Guardian Angels

My daughter, you do not live for yourself
but for souls; write for their benefit.

~Saint Maria Faustina

In this newly discovered state of my soul, I realize I am a spirit in the world. My soul is one with God and, through my spirit, I live on with duties to perform. But just what would my heavenly duty be?

I have always believed in guardian angels. Maybe now I could become one. When I was human, I was sure that I had a guardian angel. I even had a special metal charm of an angel that I cherished. Often when I talked to my angel, I felt its presence in that charm. The physical representation of an angel is what many humans seek when faith needs to be strengthened for the unseen.

I put so much trust in my charm that I panicked when I lost it a few weeks before my death I believed that was a sign. Spiritually, I knew death was coming and I embraced it. I was even excited to return here, but physically, I was depressed. I knew that my physical time was done and afraid of what might happen.

In a human body, it is natural to communicate, to touch, to love, to grow, and to have relationships with others. Without my physical body, I wondered if and how I would maintain my relationships. As a guardian angel over my family, how would they hear me? How will they know I am still present? As I journey to understanding this, I will share what I know.

People with strong faith can communicate easier, but what about those that struggle with their faith, you ask? Well, maybe that could be my special gift—to nurture faith.

I shall shadow the many guardian angels that surround this place; I shall become what one may call, an understudy.

I've always loved learning new skills, but the talent that I am surrounded by here, barely compares to nursing school or floral arranging (which were my earthly talents). There is so much activity and the attention to detail is amazing. There are groups of angels gleefully dedicated to sharing their gifts and bestowing them on others. The gift of life is merely one; there are too many to name them all. There are gifts of music, teaching, writing, parenting, patience, forgiveness, knowledge, understanding, and the greatest gift of all...love.

The details for each gift given are intertwined in the most specific way to create the most beautiful picture. It's comparable only to a giant quilt designed by God where He carefully and thoughtfully hand-planted each individual seed to grow the cotton for each exact placement in the picture that the quilt bestows. It is amazing, I am in constant awe.

Guardian angels present individual gifts as they are needed or assigned. Yes, there really are guardian angels for everyone, often times many angels for each soul. Most angels are created from the souls of spirits that chose to never experience a physical form. These are spirits that have never had a human incarnation, however, there are some that have.

Almost any spirit, whether once human or not, can become an angel by sharing a gift that they have been given by God. The catch is that they must give to the recipient out of their own free will. It is truly wonderful to watch. Once a receiving soul accepts the gift, the giving spirit rises to an angelic level. I decided I wanted to do this; try to give a gift.

Once I made the decision to share my gifts and talents with other souls, I found it difficult to get them to accept them, or use them. I tried everything I could, but nothing happened. Then I realized that, in my physical existence, I had been named an angel on earth. I distinctly understood what this meant. Memories began to flood through me, and the gifts I had bestowed in my earthly life were clear. I saw my gift of creativity given to the neighbor children as I organized arts and craft activities during summer months. I remembered giving the gift of beauty and fruitfulness in the gardens I planted and the flowers I grew. It never occurred to me that these simple things were acts of an angel. I now realize how blessed I was to have been granted these God-given gifts to share with others when I was in my physical state.

My chosen career had been nursing and I often felt like an angel of mercy as I did my earthly job. Now, I truly understand how I was gifted by God to deliver gifts of healing, peace, compassion, wisdom, and love to my patients. I realize that these gifts were accepted by my recipients and now I realize what their acceptance gave me. It was this gift that allowed me to be at peace with my earthly death. This is the gift God wants us all to accept; to let His will and His gifts flow through us.

After this revelation, I continued to be confused about why my life ended so young. I understood it was my time, but my time to do what? Wouldn't I be more acceptable as an earthly angel, freely giving the gifts I had? If I had remained in my physical body, wouldn't I be able to communicate with others? How would I communicate now? No one could see me; no one could hear me. My family knew I was around, but even their faith didn't allow me to communicate with them. What "better" things did God intend for me now?

As I questioned and allowed my spirit to fill with human emotions and confusion, another spirit came over to me. She was the first spirit, other than my family, to identify herself to me. Her name was Carmella. She was many years older than I and she was very beautiful. She was encompassed in a silver aura, that made her glow as if she was in the shadow of a spotlight.

Carmella gave me a visual of herself in human form. She fluttered her fairy like angel eyes and they glistened with inner wisdom that spoke to directly to my soul. Her heart looked as if it was made of gold. This golden glow reminded me of my special gold charm, which I had nicknamed "Carm" because, as a child, I couldn't always pronounce my words properly. Carmella was my "Carm" now. Everything was beginning to feel like carma (karma—get it?).

The energy surrounding Carmella drew us close together as all the information I needed from her flowed into me. I felt as though I was caught up in a tornado made of pure love. She told me about her earthly granddaughter, Cora, and how Cora could communicate with angels and understood many heavenly signs. Carmella knew that if I could learn and understand how this was done, then I could begin to communicate with my own family.

I was about to embark on a wild ride. It occurred to me that I was supposed to have met Cora during my earthly experience, and I never did. Well, now I am about to meet her. This was going to be so cool. I couldn't wait to talk with her, but Carmella warned me that Cora wouldn't just talk to any spirit, I would have to gain her trust. What a journey this would be, how would I get her to trust me as much as she trusted her grandmother?

3
The Psychic

*Confirmation through the spirit can
question or renew the heart.*
- unknown author

About a year before I died, I moved back home with my mother. Due to health issues, I wanted to be home, I needed to be closer to my mom. I dabbled in my favorite pastime of floral designing and I cared for the plants in the house, but time seemed to drag by.

One day, when I was in the garage tinkering with flowers, our neighbor, Agnes, stopped by to see if I was looking for a floral job. We referred to Agnes as Saint Agnes because she was a gentle and compassionate soul. Agnes had lost her husband years earlier. Everyone in our neighborhood respected and admired her. At the same time, we felt sorry that she had the lone struggle of caring for her handicapped son. Although, we felt bad for her Agnes never showed her son anything but love, compassion, and pure dedication. She surely was a saint; however, I also knew that all mothers were saints! A mother will do anything for their kids, as my mother was doing for me.

Agnes told me about the flower shop where she was working. She said the shop's owner was looking for help and that I should apply. Boy was I interested, but I just couldn't commit to any type of schedule. It was at that moment that I knew I was too sick, and the reality of dying became even more real to me. My mother encouraged me to go there and introduce myself, but I couldn't. I knew I didn't have long.

Often, during that period, I wanted to talk to my mother about my upcoming death, but I couldn't. I understood why, but I was also aware of the reality of the situation. I yearned to discuss details of my funeral and how grateful I was for everything she'd given me, but I just couldn't bear to see her sad.

At any rate, here I am now a spirit and I have discovered that Cora, Carmella's granddaughter, is the owner of that flower shop.

Traveling in my new spirit way, I see the flower shop and spend time observing Cora. It is an adorable shop—well kept, organized, and busy. The business is thriving, the flowers are beautiful, and the staff is so much fun to listen to. Cora is constantly busy designing, bookkeeping, planning, and visiting with customers. I am amazed at the speed of her work and her talent, not just with the flower arranging, but the planning and discussions with her customers. Cora welcomes each customer and listens empathically to their needs. She embraces signs from spirits quietly, as they confirm her ability to communicate with each customer.

The more I am around her, the more I know we would have been great friends while I was among the living. As a spiritual woman, she feels spirit around her and never questions it when talking with a customer. When she's alone, however it's a different story.

She feels my spirit, and even hears me at times, but mostly, she dismisses my presence. It's going to be challenging to win her friendship as a spirit, because Cora is fearful and hesitant to acknowledge me.

Over the next few mornings, I try to show my friendliness, but she doesn't accept my greetings. Instead, Cora asks for little signs---red bird to be at the bird feeder, or the ability to eat breakfast and get out the door at an exact time, or a light turning green at the intersection, or just receiving a smile from a stranger. All these signs seem easy for me to manage. I'm able to find ways to make contact with others without their consciousness knowing. A happy thought in a stranger's head can make them smile which allows a sign to be given. Yet each time I attempt to show Cora a sign, she dismissed it as a coincidence.

I needed to come up with something big. Carmella told me that Cora had been trying to get pregnant and was having some minor health problems. Cora was nervous and her faith in her doctors was not solid. She firmly believed in God's will and she trusted that God would provide, but the unknown scared her. She really needed some gifts in patience and trust. She often prayed to her grandmother for guidance and Carmella said this is where I could help, as well as learn.

My first mission! I was confident. I had been an angel of mercy on earth, so that part of my mission would be flawless, but communication with Cora and getting her to accept me and my gift of friendship is the mission that I most want to succeed at now.

I was briefed on Cora's life. When I say briefed, it wasn't like a meeting, but the information just poured into me. It is like that in heaven, when you need more information, it just flows into you. Cora is very spiritually affluent and often used signs to communicate. Recently, she had not been interpreting the signs I sent her because she did not trust me. She could feel my presence, but she blocked me out because she did not know me.

The majority of the spirits she communicated with were family, friends, saints, and God's angels that she read about. Since I was not family, nor had I been introduced to her as a human, how would she learn about me? There are no books written about me and I certainly didn't know how to write one for her to read.

Cora's spiritual trust was often on test mode because of her awareness of evil in the world. She had setup communication with the spirit world as a child. Now, as an adult, when she communicated with spirit, she would sometimes test them to confirm their righteousness. And she did this with me many times. I have learned that most spirits like Cora (a spirit having a human experience) have great faith, but they often fail to use their gift of wisdom to accept the faith.

Faith is having trust in the unseen, but accepting faith...it takes wisdom to know truth. Cora learned her truth through her family, friends, faith, and nonfiction stories, but this faith wasn't allowing her to believe in something or someone she had never heard of...and that is me. Cora's acceptance of me would be by invitation only.

I needed an invitation! I had been trying to open a door before knocking on it. Cora could hear me, but she didn't trust me. I wanted to find a way to be welcomed. We needed to be introduced.

I asked Carmella if we could get her to visit a psychic. Perhaps a psychic could translate my friendship offering. Many people find comfort and clarity through a psychic. When I was on earth, I really wanted to know more about communication with psychics. I often wondered how it worked. Carmella explained that many psychics can hear spirits because they trust and accept the gift of the Holy Spirit, which is the energy that merges all spirits into one with God. Gifted psychics communicate with individual spirits that were once human in order to teach lessons of unconditional love and help them to have closure.

31

The gift of closure, as some word it, is merely a physical trait, not a spiritual trait. Many people can't hear or feel their deceased family members' spirits because they are harvesting unaccepted unconditional love, which only allows their free will to fear the communication.

Carmella showed me one of her meetings with a psychic. This is yet another cool thing about this place; the past can be replayed as if videotaped so that lessons can be taught.

We traveled to a psychic's house. The sign by the mailbox said, "Spiritual Communicator." The driveway was short yet very wide with a large front yard covered with freshly fallen leaves. During this playback, I found myself next to a young girl standing under the overhang on the porch. We were at the side door, I tried to knock on the door, but my knuckles made no noise. We could see a woman inside her kitchen finishing the dishes from a spaghetti dinner. She looked at the door just as the young girl rang the bell. I could hear her thoughts; she said, "Just on time."

This appointment was with Carmella's niece Leslie, who arrived with her sister. I can't believe I didn't notice the sister until we were inside. As the woman welcomed them, I actually thought she was talking to me. That's when I realized she was talking to Leslie's sister. At this point, Carmella told me to just observe because if the psychic felt my energy, it could change the replay drastically.

I began to hear everyone's thoughts more clearly. The psychic's name was Annie. She politely invited Leslie and her sister to sit at her kitchen table. "Would you like some tea?" she asked as she began to pour three cups. She knew that with every new client she'd have to take some time to break the ice with hospitality and small talk while the spiritual energy filled her with knowledge.

In the meantime, I watched Carmella describe to Annie that this was her niece. Carmella guided Annie to draw a picture in her mind. The sketch showed a lady holding a baby girl and then another picture with the same lady holding another baby. The first child was older now and standing next to the lady. Carmella then quickly flashed the picture of the new baby as a grown woman who looked a lot like Leslie, but older. Then Carmella began communicating even faster showing Annie a picture of a rose with the word Rose written next to it. Carmella was looking exhausted with all these split-second reports.

Annie made small talk with Leslie in an attempt to make her comfortable. After a few moments, Annie calmly picked up a pencil and began to draw a rose in a rectangular box. She scripted the word *Rose* under it, just as Carmella was showing her. Annie asked Leslie, "Does this mean anything to you?"

Leslie responded, "Rose is my mother's name, and the license plate on her car had a rose on it with the word *rose* written under it just like that. She's had that license plate almost her whole adult life."

Visually, Annie began to see her own mother suffering, and she asked, "Is your mother ill?"

"Yes," responded Leslie. "Is she going to be alright?"

Rather than answer her questions, Annie talking to Leslie about how hard it is to lose a parent to death. Leslie began to cry. She had started the process of mourning her mother's death before it happened; this was part of her healing process. I felt bad for Leslie. Even though death is part of life, it's hard knowing your loved one is dying. I could see even more clearly how difficult it must be for my mother to accept my death. I was hopeful that, one day I'd be able to communicate with my mother. I knew that she wouldn't listen to me until she had finished grieving.

Annie continued the reading: "I am being shown a younger sister. Did your mother have a younger sister?"

Leslie responded that her mother didn't have a younger sister and that Rose was the youngest.

While this conversation was unfolding, Carmella showed Annie the letter "M" and began repeating her own name, almost shouting, "Carmella," but Annie was getting confused. She saw the letter "M" and thought it had to do with Leslie's mother, so she continued to pass along information about Rose. After about five minutes, Annie remembered the picture of the woman with two babies, and said, "Did your mom have a sister whose name began with 'M'?"

Leslie said no, but then quickly got goose bumps as Carmella bopped her on the head. She rubbed her head and exclaimed, "Oh wait....Carmella, that's mom's sister! Mom called her Carm. I actually called her Aunty M."

With that statement, Aunty M was smiling from ear to ear.

During the meeting with Annie, Carmella was able to communicate to Leslie that she was all right and happy in heaven. Annie said, "You recently had a dream about Aunty M?"

"Yes," Leslie said, rather excitedly. "I've dreamt of her many times over the years."

I was so excited to witness Annie's gift and see the delight on Leslie's face. If only I could give my mother or

Cora some confirmation. I couldn't imagine how I would get either to go to a psychic. Then I heard Annie say to Leslie, "Your aunt is asking if you could do a favor for her."

Leslie said, "Sure, what?"

Without interfering with the replay, Carmella starting chanting a rhyme, but none of us could understand it. Annie tried to repeat it: "Your aunt is singing a rhyme, and it sounds like ...Coralinamoralinaangelinatina, almost gibberish. It is similar to the Banana FoFanny song."

Annie realized that Leslie's Aunty M was saying a rhyme with names mushed together. "Does the name Angelina mean anything? What about Cora, Corrina, or Caroline?" Annie began reciting other names that could fit.

Leslie stopped her at Cora, and said that she had a cousin named Cora.

Carmella quietly said to Annie, "I am thinking about her, tell her."

Annie quickly and very passively said to Leslie, "Well, Aunty M is thinking about her, you should tell her."

37

Carmella winked at me and said, "Cora will understand this and know that everything will be all right."

I smiled back amazed at how the psychic world gathered all their communication and translated it. Earthly life really is hard. Remembering things is difficult and trying to learn facts from thin air seems almost impossible, unless you are in this spiritual state.

Just as I was thinking this, I could feel Annie sensing my presence. She was answering my earthly questions to Leslie. She told Leslie and her sister how she became psychic and how she had always felt the presence of angels and spirits. She had listened to these voices and followed them in her personal life for years.

She didn't share that she heard voices to many people, as she feared people would think she was crazy. A select group of close friends knew she had a gift and they would often call her for advice. Annie tried to guide them the best she could. She never told them how she knew certain things and they never questioned.

Carmella explained to me that many people, including Cora, have this gift, which, at different times in life, becomes more clear. "Cora," she said, "is afraid to accept it unconditionally because of crazy judgments."

Annie continued to explain to Leslie, and to me, that she didn't really "hear" voices; it was just that she felt the voice and could communicate with it. She was able to communicate by feeling an individual spirit's energy and understanding what images displayed in her mind. The images often tell a story, similar to watching a movie clip or reading a letter. Words and images vibrate off a spirit's energy into Annie's thoughts. Many spirits will use images that the psychic can relate to, like Carmella did when she showed Annie's own mother suffering.

Cora's spiritual communication is a lot like that; however she often took the messages and translated them to herself. She had trouble understanding that she was not the recipient of the message. Annie knew, when she saw her own mother suffering, that it was a message for Leslie, not herself. Cora struggles with this clarity, which is why some of the messages she receives don't make sense and begin to scare her.

Most psychics don't usually know exactly what they are translating, but the message is clear to the recipient and that is what psychic reading is about.

Annie began doing spiritual readings for others about twelve years earlier, after she received a clear sign. As she was lying in bed one evening, having an ordinary conversation with her spirit guides, she asked how she could help a friend that she knew was going to have some trouble.

Annie wanted to prepare her, but was aware that she couldn't give unsolicited information. This particular friend knew that Annie had a special gift. At least she believed that Annie believed that she had a gift. Realistically, this particular friend silently thought Annie might be crazy.

Annie thought about this friend, and about the friends that had encouraged her to offer readings as a business, but, at that time, she still had doubts and fears. She asked her spirit guides to send her a sign if this was really her calling. She rarely asked for signs to validate herself, but she needed to know if she was actually called to do this line of work on earth.

Within an hour after she had fallen asleep that evening, her phone rang and woke her up. The person on the other end of the phone was crying and asking for her help. As Annie began to wake up, she realized that this was the same person who was on her mind before she fell asleep.

The woman apologized to Annie for calling so late, and she admitted that she had not believed in Annie's gift before. She said, "If you truly have this gift, would you be willing to meet with me and give me a reading?"

Annie was shocked. This had to be her spirit's sign to her, and she agreed to meet with the woman the following day. Annie later opened her psychic business and receives a good many clients strictly through word of mouth.

Even though most of her clients are referrals, she's still hesitant to speak freely about what she does. She realizes that the people who seek her out are open to the spirit world, therefore she can share her information without worry that she is meddling in another's business. She also knows that there are many people who aren't open to her gift, and some of them might try to discredit her gift or even try to harm her. That is the reason she does her psychic readings in her own home.

Having people come to her home allows them to see that she lives normal like they do. I admit that, when I was on earth and thought about the life of a psychic, I imagined that their homes were lined with beaded wallpaper and full of hocus-pocus stuff. At least in Annie's case, it wasn't. She was very down to earth and normal looking.

4

The Scare

If you can imagine it, you can create it.

If you can dream it, you can become it.

~William Arthur Ward

Learning patience is God's will and Cora understood this. Many nights, as she prayed, she would call on individual saints and relatives to help her be patient. Patience is a heavenly gift and, like most heavenly gifts, it needs nurturing.

One particular night when she was expressing her need for patience in accepting God's will, she asked for all the saints and angels to help her. She didn't know what that entailed, but her religious upbringing had strengthened her faith to trust that her will was God's will. Anyone who calls on an angel or spirit is heard, and knowing that Cora possessed the gift to communicate, many spirits wanted to help.

The number of spirits Cora began to hear from overwhelmed her. She had always played safe, only trusting spirits she knew. Although, spiritually, Cora trusted that God would only send her guides that would keep her safe, her humanity made her doubt that.

The next day, her godmother Maria called Cora to pass along the message Leslie received at the psychic reading. Carmella and I were hopeful that hearing from a family member would help Cora build trust in herself and what she was going through. Unfortunately, getting the message to Cora was a heavy task. In the blink of an eye, Carmella showed me why a simple message transmitted in the spirit world can take so long to be communicated.

Apparently, Leslie hadn't felt comfortable calling Cora because she didn't think the message sounded that important; and what was she going to say—"Your grandmother came to me in a psychic reading and she wanted you to know she's thinking of you?" Leslie thought it was weird and she also feared that Cora would think she was crazy for going to a psychic.

Leslie was several years older than Cora. Now that they were grown, they only saw each other at weddings and funerals; and they'd never really spoken on the phone. Because of these obstacles, this message was passed on through heavenly intervention via a series of intentionally orchestrated coincidences.

Act One, as they would say on Broadway: Leslie commuted to work by bus every morning. She would have a friend drop her off at the bus station, grab a cup of coffee at the café there, and read the paper while waiting for the bus to begin loading. On this particular day, Carmella's daughter, Maria, happened to be dropping her husband off at the same bus terminal. Her husband also took the bus every morning, however, he usually drove himself and parked his car at the terminal. Today, Maria drove him as his car was in the shop to repair a dent in the bumper that he'd received a few weeks earlier in a fender bender.

As Maria began to pull away from the station that morning, she noticed Leslie sitting on a bench reading. It had been almost five years since they had last seen each other. Even though Maria was running late for work, she rather spontaneously decided to stop and say hello.

When Leslie saw Maria approaching, she was flooded with emotions. She stood and they embraced in a warm hug. Maria asked, "How is your mom doing?" Maria knew exactly how she was doing, as she had just seen her the day before.

Leslie told her about the test she'd just had and that they were still awaiting some results. Maria knew that it really didn't matter what the results were going to say, because it was just a matter of time; Leslie knew this, too.

Leslie's eyes began to fill with tears as she said, "I never knew how hard this would be. I know it's in God's hands, but I don't think Mom is ready to go. She seems so scared to die and that scares me."

Maria said, "Don't be scared, she will be fine. I know it is hard to lose a parent, I've lost both of mine and it is tough, but we have to trust God, and your mom will when its time."

"Thanks Maria," Leslie said, feeling a sense of relief, "not just for those words, but also for visiting Mom so often. I'm sorry we keep missing each other, but I'm glad to know Mom has company when I can't be there."

"By the way, Maria, can I tell you something kind of weird?" Leslie asked.

"Sure, nothing is too weird to me. What's up?"

Leslie asked, "Do you still see Cora?"

Maria nodded. "All the time. Why?"

Leslie told Maria about her reading. She also told her that she wasn't sure if she truly believed in psychics, but that Annie had described her dream exactly. Maria admitted that she was a bit skeptical when it came to psychics, too, but it was comforting to know that her mom was watching over them.

"Cora will be thrilled to hear this news. We just talked the other night about communication from the grave. I think this will help her." Maria added, "Thanks for sharing, I'm sure our moms will be happy to be together again. Before walking away, Maria said, "If you need anything, call me."

As Maria left the bus terminal, she could feel her mother's presence. She talked with her in the car and was so thankful that God had motivated her to go out of her way to talk with Leslie. She knew it was more than a coincidence that she had to drive her husband to the bus station that day. She felt great and hoped that Cora would begin to feel this good, as well.

Cora placed a lot of trust in her godmother. Many times, when she became fearful of the spirits that surrounded her, she turned to Maria for guidance. Maria knew that Cora wanted to become a mother, but it wasn't happening for her just yet. Maria understood this frustration, for it took her over ten years to conceive. Maria recalled the many nights when Cora would visit. She talked about her desire to have a child and described herself as being in a dark tunnel. She knew there was a light at the end, but she just couldn't see any flickering.

I could totally understand this analogy because, when I was dying, I also knew there would be a light at the end of the tunnel, but I wanted a sign. As it got closer, I was sent a special angel to guide me and now I was hopeful to be that special angel to guide Cora. But first I had to gain her trust.

Later that day, Maria went into the chapel and prayed to the Holy Spirit to guide her on whether or not she should call Cora. I was excited that Maria might pass the message to Cora. While in the chapel, the Holy Spirit reminded Maria about the first time she was visited by a spirit. She had been nine years old and lying in bed when Jesus appeared to her and sat on her bed. She barely recalled the conversation, but the unconditional love that had encompassed her that day, remains with her today. She knew that, as a godmother, she was expected to provide unconditional support to her godchildren.

She began to think about Cora's spiritual journey and how to engage the Holy Spirits. She knew that many spirits work through the Holy Spirit and we all are one; one day this will make sense to you, too. Maria reflected on Cora's struggles yet admired her constant faith. With that thought, Maria convinced herself that Cora's faith would help her accept the message.

At the time Maria was in the chapel (which I should label as Act Two, for this Broadway production) Cora was at the doctor's office. The doctors had just told her that they would like to schedule a procedure to further investigate her infertility. Cora was nervous. Some of the things that they would check for included cancer and that was a word that truly scared her. Her life flashed before her eyes; she began to mourn her own life and fear not ever being able to have a family. She also began to think about what it would be like to embrace her grandmother again in heaven, and it all seemed bittersweet. As she walked out of the doctor's office, her cell phone rang, it was her godmother.

Before Maria dialed Cora's number, she began to have some doubts because she didn't want to scare her. She wanted this message to comfort her. So did we.

When she saw the caller ID, Cora was comforted that Maria was calling her at that exact moment. "Hi Aunt Maria," she answered in a relaxed voice.

"Hi Cora, are you busy?" asked Maria.

"No, what's going on?" Cora responded.

Maria chuckled. "I have a funny story to tell you and it just might make you smile."

"Well, I could use a good story and a smile. Enlighten me

Maria began to tell the story of her bumping into Leslie at the bus station. Half way through the story, Cora's jaw just dropped, her heart began thumping out of her chest, and she felt as if she was covered with goose bumps.

Carmella explained to me that these were signs of confirmation of our spirit. As Maria finished the story, Cora swallowed hard and began to tell Maria what had happened only minutes earlier.

"Do you think Grandma is trying to tell me I'm dying? Do I have cancer?" Cora asked hesitantly.

Carmella and I began to laugh, Oh my, that was the furthest message we wanted to send. Even if that were the case, we certainly would not have gone to a psychic to send that message!

Maria calmed Cora down and I tried to console her by saying, "That's not it; you are okay." But Cora tuned me out. I said over and over, "It's going to be okay." I gently placed my hand on her shoulder as a gesture of compassion. This was the first time Cora truly sensed my presence without fear, and I began to introduce myself to her. "Hi, don't be scared, my name is Rhealynn and I'm here to help. I'm here to be your guardian angel."

As I did this, she was still talking to Maria. She said that she still felt many angels and spirits around her, but didn't know which ones were safe to trust. Maria told her to lean on her faith and trust the voice of God. What great advice. I wish all children could have an encouraging godmother like this.

Carmella reassured her that she could trust us. I repeatedly said to Cora, "You can trust me. I am here to help you. Trust Rhealynn

When Cora heard this, she said to her godmother, "If I were to trust everything I heard, then apparently my angels are advising me to take Ritalin or Prozac or something!" She laughed. "Yeah that must be it! I need meds. I'm going crazy."

At that point, Maria told Cora that she wasn't crazy. They discussed the mystics of the old days and how talking with the dead and spirits was more commonplace then. Cora said there seemed to be a fine line between physics and psychosis. She wondered where she fit in.

That's when Maria informed her that she was not psychotic and she probably could be considered a mystic. She advised her not to over-analyze it and just accept it. But Carmella and I knew that Cora was reading too much into the message and even mistranslating the message if she was thinking she needed Ritalin! She needed Rhealynn.

5

The Signs

There is a force, a quickness that is translated through you into action. If you block it, the world will not have it...Keep the channel open.

~ *Martha Graham*

"Carmella, thank you for showing me how the psychic works. I wish we could get Cora to go, or even my mother, but I don't think that either is going to happen. How are we going to be trusted again?"

"There is another way," Carmella said with a proud look on her face. "Cora's mother can help us. She will hear me when she prays. She will understand."

Cora's mother, Johanna, prayed daily and had conversations with many saints and with God directly. Over the years, her faith in spiritual advice peaked and she often shared it with her family. Of course, some thought she was crazy, but most accepted her for her beliefs.

I watched as Johanna sat on her couch, reading her prayer books. She closed her eyes when she heard Carmella's voice and they held a conversation in thoughts. Carmella said, "Johanna, your daughter is being stubborn, she is afraid that she is imagining me and you know that I would never scare her. I love my Cora and I need her to trust me."

Johanna agreed with her, responding, "Oh Carmella, it is good to hear from you and I know you wouldn't scare her, but I know that voices from beyond can make one feel crazy. Look at all I have been through. It's easy to understand why Cora is fearful. I will talk to her."

"Thank you," said Carmella.

Johanna immediately dialed Cora's number.

Cora had just finished wrapping a bundle of flowers for a customer.

"How beautiful," the woman said, beaming with excitement. "It's just what I had in mind. Thank you, Cora."

"You are very welcome, Mrs. Doogle. Now go hug that new grandbaby and come show me pictures."

"Oh, I will," Mrs. Doogle said as she left the shop.

Just then, the phone rang. Cora answered professionally, then "Oh, Hi Mom. How are you today?" The two women talked briefly about the shop's activities, then Johanna said to Cora, "Listen, I talked with Grandma today and I think she really does want to talk with you. She told me that she enjoys communicating with you and you can trust her."

Cora responded, "Oh Mom, I'm trying to trust her, but somehow I can't hear her clearly. I'm thinking that maybe I need a psychic to help me translate her. But, if I do that I might be giving into the evil spirits."

"Oh, Cora," Johanna said, "I once thought that psychics could be evil, too. I could never go to one, so I understand your dilemma. But you must trust yourself and your grandmother. Grandma is your family. Try to remember some of the conversations you've had with her in the past when she was alive and after she died. You trusted her then and you should be able to trust her now."

"But, Mom, what will people think if I tell them I am really talking with my dead grandmother. I mean I really can hear her; it's not just me thinking I hear her."

Johanna responded. "You don't need to tell anyone that you hear your grandmother. No one needs to know if you don't want to share it. But I do think that you should simply have a conversation with her."

Cora trusted her mother and knew she was right. After all, Johanna didn't always share the communication she had with God with anyone besides her. Cora believed her mother really did have a special connection with God. She witnessed several miracles that she had prayed for. Johanna often did novenas (a prayer said on consecutive days). She would say the novenas at other people's request. Once she prayed for a young boy who had a brain tumor and when she finished her novena, she learned the tumor had disappeared. The doctors said it had just shrunk on its own, but Johanna believed it was the power of many people praying.

Johanna's prayerful life was very serious and very devotional. Many times, whatever situation she prayed for received an answer. Cora, her family, and their friends often called on Johanna's prayers; especially when it came to finding lost articles. Johanna had a special connection to Saint Anthony, the Catholic patron saint of lost things. Her faith in St. Anthony has been unshakable. Once she lost a half-carat diamond ring in a parking lot, and, after an hour of searching with St. Anthony, she found it. There are many other impressive miraculous situations like this one.

When Cora got off the phone with Johanna, she began to talk to Carmella, but in a nonchalant way. She said, "Listen Grandma, I hear you. You didn't have to go telling my mother on me. I want to communicate with you, but I'm fearful. Why do I feel scared of you? I sense danger....I sense something not right, is it with you? Is someone else trying to tell me something for someone else? I don't know how I can have these conversations with you. Am I truly crazy when I hear you, or do I need Ritalin or Prozac? And, God forbid you appear to me, I will just freak out completely."

Carmella embraced Cora and snickered a little. "Don't worry Cora, I won't appear to you. I don't want to scare you. I just want to be with you. I can help prepare you. Relax." Carmella continued her efforts to comfort Cora as she sat quietly in her office trying to figure out what to do. She wanted to feel close to her grandmother again, but she also realized that, in order to trust that this really was her grandmother, she would have to acquire proof.

She decided that she should set-up rules so that when a sign came to her, she would have valid proof that it was her grandmother. One rule was that the sign had to be positive, loving, and not an ordinary coincidence. A second rule was that it would have to be some sort of sign to let her know that it was okay to continue this business of talking to spirits. With those rules, she was ready.

What happened next had to have been in the planning for years, which shows that God knows and orchestrates everything. Before I begin to tell you about what happened to Cora next, I must tell you how her day at work had been going before her mother called.

When she arrived at work, there were two messages from unsatisfied customers. Both had ordered arrangements with roses that were wilting very quickly. Cora felt bad about the flower condition and quickly handled the complaints properly. After she dealt with the customers, she called her rose supplier to see if they had any other issues with the roses. They hadn't, which meant that the roses Cora's employees delivered hadn't received the proper conditioning. She'd been pretty busy that morning and must have been negligent. She felt awful that this process was overlooked as it was standard procedure.

If it had only been one complaint, the problem may lie in conditions within the customer's house, but two complaints with the same batch of roses meant either the grower shipped a bad product or the shop's processing was compromised. Since it seemed to be the latter, she was naturally upset because she took pride in her shop's professionalism and thoroughness. This could not happen again, she thought.

Cora was in her office having a conversation with Carmella. The shop was very busy. The designers were creating, the sales staff were taking orders over the phone, and a few customers were browsing. Allison, the shop's manager, had greeted the customers and was waiting to assist them, when the front door opened. In walked an elderly man. Allison said, "Good Afternoon Sir, and welcome, how can I help you today?"

The gentleman replied, "I'm actually here to speak with the owner. Is the owner available?"

Allison, ever the call-screener asked, "Can I tell her who you are?"

He answered firmly, "No, I would just like to speak with her now."

Allison hesitantly poked her head into Cora's office. She knew Cora was having "one of those days" and she really didn't want to disturb her, but she knew this man wanted only her.

"Excuse me, Cora," Allison said shyly, noticing that Cora was obviously deep in thought. "There's a gentleman that would like to speak to you. I tried to help him, but he insists on talking with you."

Cora looked at Allison with exhaustion and dismay, "I don't know if I want to handle another complaint; three in one day…what the heck is going on?"

Allison reminded her, "You don't know that he's going to complain. Take a deep breath, now. You handled the others fine, and this will be okay, too."

"I hope so," Cora said as she walked over to the customer.

Cora introduced herself to the gentleman.

Gesturing to the fact that there were customers in the shop, he asked, "Is there a more private area where we could talk?"

"Certainly, follow me." Cora lead him to a private consultation area about ten feet away. Her employees flashed looks of empathy; no one had a good feeling about this private talk, least of all, Cora. She quickly said a little prayer to her grandmother to give her strength and asked for a sign. Once they had relative privacy, Cora looked into the man's twitching blue eyes with compassion and genuine concern. "How can I help you today?" she asked.

His eyes pierced through her, as he leaned on his cane and said, "Well, I have done business with your shop for many years and I have to tell you that I recently ordered a flower arrangement to be sent to my sister while she was recovering from surgery at the local hospital."

Cora felt her stomach begin to knot up and her anger was building. She took a lot of pride in her flowers. Sure, she had been busy lately, but she really cared about the quality and condition of her flowers and designs. If his complaint was going to be about the same roses, then maybe it was a bad batch. Although he did say that he'd recently sent flowers. At his age maybe last year was recent.

Her mind raced, as she scolded herself and doubted her profession. She wanted to cry, but she remained professional as she listened to the man tell his story. He became animated as he said, "I want you to know that my sister told me those flowers were the most beautifully designed arrangement she'd ever received."

"What?" Cora was dumbstruck. Even a passing customer smiled as they also thought a complaint was being delivered. A few nearby employees breathed sighs of relief.

The man began to shake his cane gently. "Believe me, my sister is no spring chicken. She has received lots of flowers in her days, and for her to say that it was the best she ever got, was definitely a tribute to you, your staff, and your shop. She still has the card, which says the name of your shop on the back side and she tells everyone about the arrangement. She even saved the basket and bow."

This certainly was not the first time that Cora or her shop had received a compliment. Many thank you notes from happy customers hung on the wall in her office, and many customers had called or stopped in to pay compliments. This compliment today, however, was exactly what she needed—a good sign.

Carmella nudged me and said, "Just wait until she really gets her sign."

Cora smiled at the gentleman and thanked him. She said, "You certainly have been heaven-sent today. I needed a boost and I really appreciate you taking the time to come here."

Before the elderly man walked out the door, he turned to Cora and said, "Listen young lady, I just want you to know that I will always do my business here and, as long as I'm around, I'll tell everyone of the great work you do."

After he left the shop, the employees were all buzzing about how animated the man had been and how wonderful it was that he stopped by.

Allison turned to Cora and said, "Well, that was a really nice sign."

Cora smiled and knew that, yes, it was a sign.

Later that afternoon, Cora talked more with her grandmother, and began to test her. Carmella told me that she didn't mind being tested because she knew that by testing her, Cora's soul would learn to trust more. Gaining this trust was going to be based on unconditional love and rules that the conscious mind must create in order to allow the soul to travel to the bridge of trust.

That night, Cora laid in bed and pleaded to her grandmother not to come to her in a dream that night. "I don't think I can handle you appearing to me right now, not in a dream, and certainly not in an awake vision. If I wake up and you are standing above my bed, I think I'll have to drive myself to the mental hospital."

Carmella laughed at her granddaughter's plea. First of all, she couldn't just materialize her spirit and appear to her. It just wasn't possible. She was a spiritual soul without access to a human body. She could only refer to pictures of herself when she was on earth. She was different now. If she appeared to Cora in a dream, she would be able to tell Cora more, but she knew tonight wasn't the night. She did not want to frighten her or lose her trust.

By the way, I totally agreed with Cora about the vision thing. When I was on earth, I'd heard of people seeing dead people, like the movie, "The Sixth Sense," and I thought they were probably crazy or needed meds. I always assumed that I'd see dead people when I died and that is what happened.

The next day, as Cora was driving her car to work, she continued to test and question Carmella. She asked for signs to confirm she wasn't imagining all this. She asked for a light to go green quick, she asked to see an airplane fly by, she asked for her phone to ring, she asked to spot a blue car, and she even asked to see a tiny white dog. Each time, when she'd get the sign, she'd smile, but then discredit them by saying that it was too likely that it would have occurred. So she wanted to make it harder. She said, "Grandma, if this is really you, then I need a sign that only I will know, I'll be vague, but it has to remind me directly of you or Grandpa instantly. It could be a song, or whatever, but you gotta do this." Then Cora began changing radio stations frantically searching for a sign.

Carmella knew she had to come through, so she got Cora to look up at a billboard on the side of the road. Cora stopped the car dead in its tracks. Thankfully, no one was directly behind her on the road. She froze as she read the billboard. It was an advertisement for a company she hadn't heard about in years. It was the company that her grandfather worked for his entire life. Cora was surprised to see that the company still existed; it looked to be doing well.

Cora looked at that sign for a long time. She could hear her grandmother laughing and saying, "Well, here's your darn sign, you wanted a sign, well, how about that? A twenty-by-thirty foot billboard. Now that's a sign!" Carmella sounded sarcastic as she told Cora, "I was going to use a little street sign, but you probably would have missed it."

Cora laughed and thanked her grandmother.

6

Family Gifts

For those who dwell in the world and desire to embrace true virtue, it is necessary to unite themselves together by holy and sacred friendships. By this means they encourage, assist, and conduct one another to good deeds.
~Saint Francis de Sales

In her family's library, Cora was guided to material she needed in order to continue expanding her faith in herself and in us. Wisdom could only be granted with work. Angels cannot just give out the answers. One must be willing to look for them—do the research. Cora thumbed through many books on angels, the lives of saints such as, St. Dominick, St. Theresa, St. Mary, Jesus, and subjects such as purgatory. She also read from the Bible.

Within each book, we highlighted what we wanted her to know. This particular evening, her mother walked in and questioned what she was doing.

"I don't really know, Mom," she replied. "I feel this urge to look for something. I know that some spirit is trying to communicate with me, but I'm not sure if it is safe. I'm reading about purgatory and it sounds scary. I don't even want to believe it exists."

Johanna explained to Cora that she, too, went through this. Johanna told her daughter to be careful who she talked with about having spiritual conversations because she would need the proper guidance.

Cora asked, "Who did you trust when you were having revelations brought to your attention?"

Her mother's response did not surprise her. "God. If you ask him, he will answer you. I questioned God about purgatory too and He explained it to me. I really had an issue with 'limbo'. I did not understand why God would create such a place."

I had heard of limbo when I was on earth. It was supposedly a place where all unborn babies or unbaptized babies went upon death.

"It didn't seem fair that these babies couldn't get into heaven," Johanna said. "But God answered me when I asked."

Cora's eyes grew wide when she asked, "What did he say?"

"He said, 'Johanna, why do you call me mean for creating limbo? I did not actually create limbo; earthly people did. Just as I created the earth, I did not name Massachusetts. You earthly people put names on all these places. As far as limbo is concerned, a place does exist where unborn babies and unbaptized people go, but I allow everyone into the kingdom of heaven. My kingdom has many rooms, just as your own home does. For even in heaven, there is a time, a place, a season, and a reason for everything. No one has to suffer here, nor there; I baptize everyone as they are entered into heaven. For all the crying

73

out loud people do, I hear their pain and heal them, however not all are open to this healing while in human form. Crying cleanses the soul and that is exactly what I do, clean and purify the souls as they make their way home to me. That is why the rain on earth falls; when it rains I clean every soul and give them exactly what they need for them to enter my heavenly kingdom.'"

I will tell you that this is how God can speak—sounding like an angry teacher—but you instantly understand as you begin to feel submerged in love and forgiveness. That is what I felt when I first arrived here. Instantly, he washed through me, like baptism, purifying the soul. As humans, we can wash our bodies, but our soul can only be washed in God's unconditional love.

Cora understood what her mother was saying. She knew God's love was unconditional, and she knew that calling her cousin Leslie to find out more information about that psychic reading would not violate God's trust and hopefully it would help give her clarity to accept the process of communicating with me as a spirit.

Cora picked up the phone. "Hi, Leslie. Sorry to bother you, but I wanted to know more about the message you gave to my Aunt Maria. Maria told me you visited a psychic."

Leslie repeated the details of her psychic reading to Cora and said, "If you want to get a reading, I would go with you. I recommend Annie. I have met with her a few times over the years and I trust her."

Cora thought about Leslie's statement before saying, "I don't know; I want to trust my own faith and don't want to test it with a psychic, but I'm curious, since I often feel I'm imagining things. But I know I'm not. I have my own communication with spirits, and I don't need a psychic to spook me."

"I don't think you would get spooked. Maybe this would just confirm your imaginings. She is very gifted and I think you would get clarity," said Leslie.

Cora responded, "I do believe that some people are gifted and that they have more clarity with spirit than me, but I still think I'd get spooked."

Leslie tried to tell Cora that speaking with a psychic was not spooky. She said, "You know, Cora, I love Auntie M so much and I communicate with her all the time. Talking with Annie helped give me peace of mind. I believe Auntie M wanted me to understand that my mother would be okay. Mom has a lot of fear about dying and knowing that her sister will be there for her when she crosses over is very comforting to me."

Carmella told me that this is true. Annie wasn't trying to scare anyone; and she wasn't delivering the news that Leslie's mom was dying. That news was already known. She was only reassuring and comforting Leslie.

Leslie continued, "Auntie M would never scare us, so I hope you don't think that. When Auntie M said she was thinking of you, I believe it was her way of saying she is with you, too. I didn't know how to tell you that because it seemed a little weird to call you out of the blue with information like that. I hope you understand. I truly believe that your grandmother is our guardian angel."

Cora agreed. She thanked Leslie for talking with her. Before they hung up, Cora told Leslie she would pray that her mother have a peaceful passing.

I hoped one day my mother would understand this, I wanted to be their guardian angel, and guide them through troubling times. I had tried to communicate with my family, but I wasn't as good as Carmella. I was frustrated with the blessing to know that I am now part of this infinite energy. I am all knowing and capable of translating, yet unable to be understood.

Carmella began to show me other ways she communicated with her other family members. She said that her main mission for her family is to provide safety for them. She explained, "If a family member calls on me through prayer, I can guide them. However, it can be frustrating because all I can do is guide them. They don't have to listen, as we have seen."

Carmella showed me some occasions where she assisted her family. Her sons had always been burdened with grief over their father's sudden and early death, so she prayed to God to give them deeper faith so that wisdom would keep them from suffering like their father did. She explained that by praying to God, He gives her the ability to give gifts to her family directly, but sometimes, he provides other spirits and angels, to help.

She showed me how the gifts of patience, faith, and hope led her son-in-law and daughter to see what a blessing it was to lose his job after twenty-five years. With her gifts, she was able to communicate to them that it didn't matter what kind of job a person held, as long as they could provide for their family. She explained; "Every job one earth is important, whether you grow the wheat, bake the bread, bag the bread or deliver the bread. Each job has its reward and each if part of God's plan." They were reminded that whenever a door closes, another will open.

7

Understanding

*There are great souls who practice every sort of
mortification from childhood, but I am not like
them. All I did was to break my self-will, check a
hasty replay, and do little kindnesses without
making a fuss about them.*
~*Saint Therese of Lisieux*

The human ego is one of the hardest barriers to cross
when it comes to communication. Before a soul chooses to
continue his journey through earthly life, he is given free
will. As a human being, we are born with a brain that holds
the conscious and the unconscious minds. The conscious
mind controls the ego, whereas the unconscious mind
controls what we cannot see—our heartbeat, our blood flow,
our soul's true identity. Every soul begins life with the gift
of free will to experience life when in the physical form.
When a soul freely chooses to experience a physical life,

what they do with that time is hopefully good and loving, so that when the physical experience is over, the spirit is enriched. People were not created to be perfect and many mistakes are made on earth, which is why the miracle of the gift of forgiveness was created.

Before I died, I was not the most perfect human soul, but upon entering heaven, my soul was washed clean. Just as God had described to Johanna, the gift of forgiveness not only forgave my faults, but in some cases, helped me to understand why I did what I did. Forgiveness is important to obtain in order to purify the soul and truly connect with your oneness to heaven.

As an angel in training, which I consider myself, I have witnessed many suffering souls receiving the gift of forgiveness. I have seen that the moment a person expresses a need for forgiveness, that is the moment when God sends angels of grace to console and heal them. However, on a human level, forgiveness is not always that instantaneous because of the choice of free will. Forgiveness can only be received by a soul willing to accept it. Free will constantly causes conflict between accepting what one knows is truth and actually believing it.

Souls experiencing life in the physical form have many choices, thanks to the free will God gave to us. Being human limits the ability to merge free will and God's will for many people, causing regret. The regrets are always forgivable, as the lessons they bring become part of the human experience.

When one realizes that they have misinterpreted a message or sinned, as some think of it, they need forgiveness. This prompted Cora to ask, "How can a soul receive forgiveness if they do not even know they were wrong?"

Carmella responded: "That is the gift you receive when you cross over. What was wrong is right now for you. As spirits having a human experience, we are destined to make mistakes along our journey, however it is in those mistakes that allow for God's unconditional love to guide the proper lessons for our life's purpose."

Cora understood what Carmella said, however, I needed more information. "What about having to ask to be forgiven? On earth, in the church, you have to ask for forgiveness in confession. Can't you just be forgiven by asking?"

"Of course," Carmella said. "You've seen the angels sent to console and heal. If you are asking why the church offers confession as a formal way of forgiveness, the answer is to teach the gift. The Catholic Church is just one of many ways to teach faith. People need structure; people need rituals in order to remember the truth."

Carmella continued, "This ritual of confession was created because many souls need to confess their faults to someone. Remember when you were human; thoughts in a brain are not as clear as they are here. We know that all souls are not created alike; they are only created like God. To hear oneself confess out loud, allows for an individual to hear their own need to be forgiven. Then, not only does God hear them, but they hear their own remorse. This allows them to feel God's love and forgiveness and to begin to heal themselves."

Cora continued to speak to Carmella. She could feel my presence and even hear me joining in the conversation. I was amazed at how relaxed she was. This was a very trusting moment. "Ok, but Carm, if confession forgives your sins, then why are we given penance?"

Carmella answered, "Penance is just a Catholic term. It is a healing gesture that allows the human soul or the human mind to understand grace. The human mind often will over-analyze situations therefore blocking the simplicity of forgiveness."

"All right, I get all of that," Cora said, "but what about the punishment penance; you know when you have to say ten Hail Mary's or donate to the poor, or pray for others? How are these things healing gestures?"

"These so-called punishments, as you word it, are healing gestures to get you back on the right path," Carmella explained. "Many punishments that you were given are just to redirect you. Cleaning your room, not watching TV, or sitting still in a time-out are all examples of lessons used to help you refocus your gifts. Praying, feeding the poor, cleaning, sleeping, and even silence are all good things."

"Well, I have to ask, since I'm still in my earthly existence, why, then, once I ask for forgiveness and do my penance, do I not always feel healed and forgiven?"

"Again, free will makes the distinction. On earth, you must choose to accept the forgiveness. Once you cross over to the spiritual world again, you no longer have free will; all you have is God's will, which is the will you search for your entire earthly existence," Carmella responded. "This is what Jesus' message was all about."

To be honest with you, before I made the transition back here, I would never have understood this. I hadn't really believed in Jesus, but now I understand that his life is a story, like all of ours. Jesus' story is exceptional as it has held through time, and only God can make that happen. Whoever needs to believe or wants to believe in Jesus can and will be comforted. Every soul sent to earth is sent from God, yet, only few remember that. God came to earth as Jesus to remind us that we all have a mission, we just need to remember it.

Jesus never forgot his mission, as he had no option to forget. He knew he was created by God, and one with God. Most souls only remember that they are one with God when they cross over and merge into spirit.

As I understand it, God was frustrated with his creation of man and the fact that he gave him free will. He thought about ending the world many times, but he couldn't destroy his entire creation. And he couldn't destroy the gift of free will because then the journey to wisdom would be lost. Free will meant that people did not have to use their God-given gifts, and that was okay with God, but misuse of the gifts is what really upsets him.

God knew when he created with the gift of free will that this would bless and frustrate all souls. He then created an offering of forgiveness so that exercising the gift of free will can be enjoyed. Without forgiveness, many can get stuck and they would never truly enjoy the journey. He needs us to accept this gift, so we can journey forward to gain wisdom and to remind us where we came from.

When He created Jesus, He sent him to walk the earth in order to remind us that we were all created in his likeness. Through living life as Jesus, he told us that He would return to the Father and with that wisdom, hope brought faith to allow belief. Jesus became our father, our brother, our friend, and our spouse.

God experienced life in the human form as Jesus, and He continues to experience life in all of us. He had a human body with a spiritual soul that was awake at every moment. Jesus' free will was only God's will, as they were one and the same. God taught people through becoming Jesus that He was a father, a son, and a spirit, just as all of us are. He came to remind us that we are all one body, and, only now as I am in spirit form, do I fully grasp that!

God is one spirit. His spirit has many forms; just as the body has many parts. This allows for individual experiences to be similar or completely different, yet always fulfilling a purpose. The purpose is to uncover our own soul and know that we are of the Father, Son, and Spirit. I am a daughter, I am a spirit, and I am a part of God's creation. The peace this knowledge brought me when I crossed over after my physical death is just a peek at the glory in heaven.

When considering the thoughts that were coming through, Cora realized that this information was being given to her from another source. "Who are you?" she asked.

I did not know how to answer that, would she hear my name or would she think she needed Ritalin again? I remained silent and prayed for guidance.

8
Visionary Revelations

That you have told God about it is enough,
He has a good memory.
~Jeanne Jagan

"Thank you for praying," Carmella said to me. "If Cora begins to doubt herself at this point, we will never communicate the wisdom she will need to continue her journey; nor will you."

Cora had been reading the book about purgatory. She questioned why this place exists if all sins are forgiven. She asked us if it is true that some souls go to purgatory. I couldn't answer. Cora was right. If all I had said was true, then how does this place exist? If all sins are forgiven, then you would have to believe there would be no need for purgatory.

I remember hearing about that place when I was on earth—a place where souls suffer for their sins, in order to receive entrance into heaven. It did not seem very God-like. So I had to ask, "What happens if a spiritual soul never accepts the forgiveness they are offered? Do they go to purgatory?"

"Well, Rhealynn, I can tell you only what you can understand." said Carmella. "Creating purgatory gives the human mind some clarity to comprehend earning forgiveness. Purgatory, or whatever you want to call it, is where souls journey to understand that they have transitioned into a life after death. Many incarnate souls forget that they are part of this eternal life, so, as their physical body dies, they do not understand why they feel so alive. This place, purgatory, as the human mind names it, is not a place of intense suffering, rather a place of waiting, repairing, and learning patience."

"Is that where I am?" I asked. "I thought this was heaven."

Carmella responded, "Heaven is everywhere, a part of everything. This particular time you're experiencing in heaven is where a soul waits to discover their legacy; to rediscover their eternal mission so they can continue their journey."

This was amazing to me! I died only to arrive back in a school; stuck in purgatory, waiting for an assignment. Carmella read my thoughts, as she responded, "No one is ever stuck here. Our will chose this for us so that we may continue to do God's will in this after life. Remember, you chose to experience life and this is where we learn why."

"Okay, then why?" I asked impatiently.

"Patience is key. Everything unfolds perfectly, you will see."

"So exactly how much time do you think I have to be in this purgatory?"

"Why use such silly human words, 'purgatory' and 'time....' Time here is not measured in hours, minutes, or even days. Five years on earth can feel like a day here, and two seconds can feel like an entire year."

"Oh, I get it; but why can't the human mind understand this?" I asked.

"It can with the right translation," Carmella said.

Cora chimed in. "You cannot always measure time by a clock."

I knew this was true. It had been only seven seconds since I crossed over, yet more than seven months have passed. All this time I have been able to rest my soul here in this place called purgatory, and begin a process to heal any suffering that occurred to my soul during my physical experience."

While here, I learned that every soul requires a different amount of healing time and receives gifts of healing in many different forms. Carmella described her healing process with the use of visual pictures to me and Cora.

Her family's faith was practiced in the Catholic Church and the Catholic Church provided a tool of offering a mass for a deceased loved one. Having a mass said for a soul that has crossed over, grants that soul's spirit a gift of healing love and wisdom. With that gift, an increase of energy is given to the spirit as those who were praying for her and to her can get help with her intercession with God. Going to Mass was just one of the many ways Carmella's family healed her. They also shared memories with each other, continued traditions after her passing, and loved her.

Cora questioned if her grandmother was healed quicker or gained more wisdom faster since Masses were said. She questioned if she should book some Masses soon for her or others.

Carmella explained, "The Catholic Church created Mass as an example to fill faithfulness. Traditions teach communication and commitment. Many families share the traditional ritual of gathering in public prayer to worship God. Traditions and rituals are physical ways to maintain community throughout every generation. It promotes faithful communication, but it is not the only way." She reassured

Cora that it was not necessary to run out and book every mass.

Cora asked, "How is it that I can communicate with you now? I mean I am not in a church and rarely do people talk about communicating with dead relatives at church."

"Our communication is based on your faith, and your commitment to receiving unconditional love. Many people cannot quiet their ego long enough to find the silence their soul yearns to hear. Churches were designed to teach this silence through the offering of a sacred location—a location that requires a soul to slow down for a time and listen."

Carmella described the action of physically going to church and how it can be rewarding to both the souls of the deceased, and the physical soul. Connecting with your soul is a gift of honor to God. It creates direct communication with him. Each prayer sent up to heaven has a destination where they are heard and answered according to God's will.

As a spiritual soul, the gifts I receive from God are only presented to me by the prayer requests I hear. I cannot choose which prayer to answer; I can only pray for guidance.

I also cannot pray for myself, as I am part of God. But through the living, my life's legacy is remembered; and with the communications of my loved ones, my soul may receive guidance and grace.

9

Obvious Simplicity

Freedom is the destiny of every human being. We become free by waking from our dreams of fear, security, blame, and guilt: by taking responsibility for acting, to the best of our knowledge with care and loving kindness that we may kindle the light of love within and by that light see our way home...and serve as beacons for others along the way

.~ Joan Borysenko, Ph.D

I have met many other spirits, and I've seen the spirits named saints in the Catholic Church, where Cora practices her faith. These souls are very close to God and connect through their earthly existence to human lives. I enjoy being with them. Many of these spirits have several angels assigned to them by God to help carry out their gifts and missions. One spirit I have been drawn to is Mother Theresa.

I had known of her when I was on earth, for she was there with me; well not in my same town or anything, but she was alive the same time I was. I have been told that she will be one of the fastest souls to reach sainthood ever in the Catholic Church. Mother Teresa, Pope John, and, well, maybe me or Carmella will all be saints at the right time.

As busy as Mother Teresa is, she still meets with Carmella and I on occasions. She shared with us that Cora and she share the knowledge that God is in everyone and therefore helping any one person is also helping God. Mother Theresa is a soul capable of small acts of kindness that leave a big impression. I have watched her silently help so many and she is humble to be acknowledged. She knew she would have to be acknowledged for sainthood in order to be validated in the Catholic Church. However, she prefers to quietly seek those most suffering and comfort them in their private needs.

Mother Teresa said, "Cora is a delicate flower whose human suffering is only manifested because her earthly influences limit her ability to comprehend clarity. Her soul ebbs and flows the clarity she seeks on a human level. Many humans suffer this way—knowing their true calling, yet questioning its validity."

Cora prayed to Mother Theresa, along with many other saints; which is how I began to meet them. As she prayed, they would come. Her calls to them were usually intended to find some clarity about me and my mission with her, which has yet to unfold for us completely.

One morning, I observed Cora in Mass praying for clarity. She looked around the church for a sign, but couldn't think of one to ask for to confirm her request. She wished that there was a candle shrine to light a prayer request at that moment. Cora is a very visual soul; seeking confirmation is solace for her gift. Communicating with saints, angels, dead grandmothers, and unknown spirits, often times made her question her path. Confirmation was a way her incarnate soul could strengthen her faith.

Carmella showed me a letter that was addressed to Cora's church. It was dated on what would have been my thirty-second birthday.

Dear Father Bill,

It would have been my privilege to teach CCD this year, however I have to decline. I feel that I would not be able to devote the time to properly prepare class lessons nor attend all the classes.

My husband & I have discussed becoming more involved with the parish, yet our careers seem to over-extend our schedules. We are hopeful to begin a family soon and therefore I am realizing that my time on council, teaching, and working at the parish needs to allow for another's placement. Our parish needs attention, as the lack of volunteers for replacement is limited, and I often hear people talk about the limited resources for guidance.

I know we briefly discussed this, and I appreciate your interest in hearing my suggestions. I understand that everyone has their own ideas about how our church should do things, and not everyone's ideas can be put into motion. I just wish to plant a seed. Only God knows what really needs to be nurtured.

1. *A 9:30 Children's Program: as I discussed with you earlier, a program could be run during the 9:30 Mass each Sunday. Parents could drop their preschool children at the parish center or in the large meeting room. Students from the Confirmation classes could watch them and entertain them with Bible stories,*

102

short religious movies, games, and various forms of religious arts and crafts; while their parents reflect uninterrupted in Mass. It might be helpful by having them not attend mass, parents would be able to focus on the mass, and the interest of where mommy & daddy were going would excite the child to become grown up like their parents one day.

2. *Educational Prayer Center: this could be installed in the foyer at each entrance. It would consist of a neatly displayed rack, either on the wall, or freestanding, filled with religious material. This might include devotional prayer cards, religious newsletters, children's Bible stories, self-help pamphlets, charitable organization information, and more.*

A volunteer from one of the CCD classes could maintain it. The maintenance would consist of straightening the racks, restocking them, removing dated material, and taking inventory of material needed. I'd suggest the Saturday and the Monday night classes could each get involved with this. This way, before and after Sunday Masses, the prayer center would be attended to.

Funding for the material could be provided by a donation center or an allowance from Sunday collections.

I feel that this Prayer Center would benefit the parish by enhancing prayer, educating children, and helping those who may not be able to ask for help. Many people have the intention to pray more often. With the help of devotional prayer cards available, it may provide the teaching. Also, it would allow teenagers and grammar school-age children to pick up material to read before mass and educate them on saints, religious groups, and even Sunday Mass. Not every child has the ability to pay attention to an entire Mass and if they are going to be distracted and read Elmo, why shouldn't we try to substitute Noah's Ark.

By the way, I do realize there is a center similar to this in the parish center; however I would guess that barely fifty percent of the church-goers would venture there to stumble upon something they may be in need of.

3. *Devotional Shrine to Saint John: A devotional candle shrine or statue of St. John could be installed to the left of the children's room. There is actually a space near the windows with an empty shelf. In order to ensure safety, candles could be lit by pressing a button instead of actual matches (perhaps electronic stimulated flames could be used). A control center would monitor the flames. Once a donation was placed in the monitor center, the button would be activated to light the candle.*

The daily donations given to light the candles would help maintain the cost to run the shrine; although the initial investment would have to be made through special funding. Perhaps someone may donate money and request the set-up as a memorial to a loved one.

I feel this would benefit our parish by creating a sacred atmosphere within the church and allow parishioners to make special intentions. During mass, other parishioners would be aware of the intentions by seeing the flame; therefore other prayers would be offered for them, along with the intentions made in our intention book located in the foyer.

Again, Father, thank you inviting my suggestions. I can be reached at the flower shop if you have any questions.
Sincerely,
Cora

Carmella shared this letter with me and explained that prayer can be much like a birthday wish, and that Cora was about to receive a sign in response to her prayer. I wanted to make these wishes come true.

Cora left mass feeling that she hadn't gotten any real sign. She had secretly wished that she could have had a personal conversation with Father Bill that morning, but he rushed out after mass and she didn't get a chance to speak with him.

Within minutes of Cora getting home, Father Bill called her. He told her he saw her at mass and wanted to acknowledge receiving her letter. Cora had forgotten about the letter. She had written in over two months earlier. Father told Cora that he had mentioned it to the council and questioned if she would approach the pastor herself with her ideas. He felt that they provided great opportunities for future planning. Cora agreed and they set up a meeting.

When Cora got off the phone, she realized that this was the sign she was looking for and she chuckled to herself. "Well, I wished to have a private personal conversation with Father; I guess it doesn't get any more personal than that." She thanked her grandmother and God for once again providing her with her confirmation.

A few weeks later, Cora met with the pastor. He listened, yet he did not feel the same way as Father. Cora argued that a church devoted to a saint should have some sort of shrine in his honor. She asked about a statue for the parking lot, a painting, something...but he wouldn't budge. He argued that it seemed old fashioned to have all these statues around.

Cora respectfully listened to him, but she didn't agree. She believed that the shrine would give the church a sense of God's warmth, but he was not open to that idea. Cora left the meeting and headed to work, feeling very disappointed.

The flower shop was busy with activity, as usual. They had a wedding the next day, so everyone was busy processing flowers. Cora quickly got to work helping Allison hand-wire orchids for a bridal bouquet. Allison had read Cora's letter when she wrote it, and not only loved her ideas, but encouraged her to send the letter. She was more than anxious to hear about the meeting.

"So, how did it go?" she asked.

"Not so well. He is old fashioned and stubborn. I don't think anything will ever happen," Cora complained.

They continued working and discussing reasons why the pastor didn't agree with the suggestions. Allison said, "Well you never know, maybe one day he will change his mind, or another pastor will come in and see that letter and take action." She even went on to remind Cora that all she was doing was planting a seed, and that it could take years for anything to grow, no matter whether the pastor liked the idea or not. She reminded Cora that it was not in her control. She said, "You were the vessel from where the idea sprung, now walk away with patience."

We liked Allison. There have been many times when we included her in communication, but today was important because Cora was being stubborn and stubbornness was a sign of earthly behavior, not spiritual communication. We also had to be patient because Carmella and I both understood Cora's frustration.

When your soul is in the physical form, you can be blind to your own knowledge at times. I remember when I was in my physical form and I got confused even though I knew I had the answers. It was when I was in the hospital for the next to last time.

The doctors had told me there was nothing more they could do for me, but I was frustrated. As a nurse, I knew my medical condition and I knew that, realistically, I was going to die soon. However I could not accept it.

I began to suffer with thoughts about dying and how I really didn't want to. I knew it was my time, but on the physical level, I didn't think it was fair. I was being stubborn and I didn't want to let go of my physical body. I have to say now that I suffer because I can't console my family and friends. I still try to console them, but they can only receive what they are willing to accept. I try to tell them how wonderful this experience is and I wouldn't nor couldn't trade it for anything.

Carmella agreed with me. We discussed all the beautiful things that we were experiencing on this journey. Believe it or not, even watching suffering isn't that bad, because we are in the position to know the reward that comes. Just as Jesus went through horrible suffering, he knew his own suffering would be worth the reward of planting the faith needed for the acceptance of life after death.

Carmella and I often want to warn others, especially our family, so they wouldn't feel so helpless and alone. There is light at the end of every tunnel, which makes it worth the risk to travel. That would be a communication issue that we were would soon struggle with, for we knew that Cora was about to have a miscarriage and, with her always looking for signs, this could be detrimental to her faith in us.

We wanted to guide her through this suffering without losing her trust in us. Even Carmella knew that, if we didn't warn her, then once it happened, she would tune us out completely. Cora was just beginning to trust me and she didn't even know me, yet.

10
Understanding the Download

Keeping a written record of major 'revelations' one receives from within one's knowingness is a fruitful exercise, as understanding is elusive and may slip into obscurity if one has not made the effort to document the understanding in detail, and refer to it as often as individual situations would indicate relevant.

~Rasha

I communicated to my mother through her dreams. Often she would awake fearful that I was in trouble. She began visiting my grave daily and she would bring flowers and cards. Most times she would stay and talk to me about how much she missed me. As she left, she would feel some sense of peace within her. During these times, my voice echoed in her thoughts, yet she still questioned if I was really near or if it was just her imagination.

I was finally given a perfect opportunity to communicate with her. Cora was at a local salon and my mother happened to also have an appointment there this particular day. With the help of other angels, we got her to overhear Cora discussing her shop's sale on purple Christmas trees. I knew that when my mother heard this, she would take notice because my last Christmas with her, I had decorated a Christmas tree in all purple. She had remarked that it was too bad the needles on the tree were green, because then the entire tree would be my favorite color.

Mom approached Cora and asked where her shop was located. She wanted to get one of the purple trees to decorate my grave.

Cora explained that her shop was just down the road, and my mother said to her, "Oh, my daughter was asked to apply for a job there a few years ago."

Cora asked, "Did she ever apply?"

"No, she didn't. She was too ill to work by then."

Cora asked, "Is your daughter's name Rhealynn?"

"How did you know that?" my mother asked, startled.

"Oh, when Agnes worked for me she had told me that she asked her neighbor Rhealynn if she was interested in working, but Rhealynn told her she was undergoing some medical treatments. How is she now?" Cora asked.

"She died in March," my mother replied with chills.

"Oh, I am so sorry to hear that," Cora said in an uncomfortable, yet empathic way.

Cora sensed me place my hand on my mother's shoulders and she followed by gently stroking my mother's back. Cora said, "Well, at least she is not suffering anymore."

"I know," responded my mother.

As they continued their conversation about my life, Cora said she wished that she could have met me. I smiled because I knew she already had.

I began to tell my mother that I was Cora's friend now. She heard that thought and told Cora, "I am sure you would have been good friends."

My mother instantly knew that this wasn't just a coincidence. I was elated. This was my moment to communicate with her.

Carmella warned me to be careful as I began to put words into my mother's and Cora's thoughts. I was hopeful that Cora's ability to translate my words would be a sign for my mother to know I was okay.

I began to tell Cora a lot of information about me so that maybe she would discuss it with my mother. Cora's thoughts raced to not only try to understand me, but to understand why she was thinking these things.

"I hope you don't mind me asking, but what exactly did Rhealynn die from?"

"She had Cystitis."

Cora made a mental note to research what that was, as she continued to empathize with my mother. "I am so sorry that you lost your daughter so young. I am sure we would have been friends. I am sorry I didn't get to meet her."

"Thank you," said mom. "She was a lot like you. You remind me of her a little."

Cora smiled and heard me say we had the same birthday day.

My mother then asked, "Can I ask you when your birthday is?"

Cora found it to be an odd question, but she quickly responded, "September seventh." As soon as that came out of her mouth, she realized it wasn't her speaking.

"That was Rhealynn's birthday also! I knew you had something in common."

Cora quickly became confused and calmly said to my mother, "I don't know why I just said that; my birthday is in January." Cora felt my spirit and could hear me! This filled me with even more energy to communicate through Cora.

Cora shrugged her shoulders and said, "Well, I guess she must have wanted me to mention her birthday so you would know she really wants you to buy the purple tree."

My mother bought the purple tree and, on her way out of the flower ship, she turned to Cora and said, "I have never been a big believer of coincidences, but meeting you today was definitely more than just a mere coincidence. I am grateful that we have met. I will be back." As she left, she looked at Cora with the eyes that saw me.

I smiled back.

Once my mother had left, Cora glanced around the shop at her co-workers and said, "What was that!?" as she fell into a chair exhausted and a little freaked out.

"Well, I think you just did a psychic reading or something," Allison said.

It was 'or something' Cora thought. She felt completely drained, yet she knew something had happened between me and my mother. She decided that she had just experienced a spiritual something. When she told Allison about her dialog with my mother earlier that day, it began to make sense to her.

"Well, I guess since Rhealynn couldn't work here when she was alive, she decided to pay us a visit from the afterlife."

Just as she said this, she remembered the day she had told her aunt that she thought she heard voices telling her she needed Ritalin. She laughed realizing that perhaps it was *Rhealynn* she heard and not *Ritalin*. Just as she made this connection, her phone rang with my mother sounding a little frantic on the other end. Allison picked up the phone and told Cora who was on the other end.

Cora hesitated, thinking, *Oh God, now this lady thinks I'm her reincarnated daughter. I don't think I want to talk to her.* She shook her head no to Allison, who simply shrugged her shoulders. However, being the polite girl that Cora was, she took the phone call.

"Hello, this is Cora"

"Oh, Cora, this is Sandy, Rhealynn's mom. I have to share something with you. I hope you don't think I am some kind of nut, but something just happened to me after I left your shop. I think you'll understand."

She was talking so fast that Cora's mind was spinning as she listened to her and to me at the same time. I shouted excitedly to her, "Listen to my mother and tell her I'm okay."

My mother didn't even wait for Cora's reply, she continued, "When my daughter was alive, she had a certain necklace that she wore everywhere. It had a special charm on it and it meant the world to her."

"This is it," I told Carmella. "I can't believe I'm doing this. My patience has finally allowed my communication to be accepted."

Of course, I knew that this was happening with the help of many other angels, but it was exhilarating to finally break through. I also found it fun to be able to be in more than one place at a time, communicating unseen.

118

Rhealynn's mother continued telling her story to Cora. "After I left your shop just now, I drove home and, as I walked from my driveway to my house, I looked down to see a sparkle. It was her charm."

This did seem unbelievable to Cora. At the same time, she was beginning to understand that she needed to communicate for me, so she just continued listening.

"Cora, I swear to you, I have looked for that charm so many times. The week before Rhealynn died, she was frantic about finding it. She said that if she found that charm, everything would be alright. We searched and searched for it. Now, this afternoon, when I returned home, I found it in my driveway." She paused and then continued, "This is no mere coincidence, I should have noticed this charm there over the summer when I planted flowers, or in the fall when I raked leaves, or even this past winter as I shoveled snow...but no, I found it now, tucked in a corner of my driveway glistening in the sunlight. How is that even possible? I truly believe it was because I met you."

Cora was amazed that she felt so calm. She explained to my mother that she appreciated the phone call because she does believe that miracles happen and this was a miracle to her. She pleasantly calmed my mother by saying, "Apparently, Rhealynn wanted you to find that charm to let you know that she is alright."

I beamed. Carmella congratulated me on my success. Suddenly, I felt a surge of energy envelop me. I was being whirled around in a tizzy of lights. "What is happening?" I asked.

"Your wish was granted." Carmella explained to me that not many angels can be heard and since I was able to communicate my dying wish to my mother, I was being given my own wings and I didn't need to shadow Carmella anymore.

As I began to understand this, I felt my spirit soaring high and I began to receive new wisdom that I didn't know existed.

Carmella was thrilled for me. She knew this part of the journey well. She had sent many signs to her family throughout the years and guided them in directions that prepared them for their experiences. Now, she knew I could do this for my family, and she also knew that I could do it for others, as well.

I began to meet other angels. There were messenger angels, soul guides, and so many others; and now I was able to be one with them.

Full of excitement, I began talking to Cora and my mom. My mom was excited and listened unconditionally, and, well Cora listened carefully to me, but questioned why I was still with her. She asked, "Alright, I did what you wanted, I let you speak through me. Why are you still with me?"

I responded that I wanted to be her guardian angel also. Cora ignored me. It was a long afternoon of silence from Cora, but mom and I had a great time looking through old photographs and hugging.

On the way home from work, Cora questioned me about the incident with my mother. I knew if I answered she would ignore it, so I directed Cora's attention to the bumper of the car in front of her. The sticker on the bumper read, "If you don't believe in guardian angels, just look over your right shoulder."

Cora laughed, but she didn't look over her shoulder. She told me that she wanted to believe she could hear me this clearly, but she definitely did not want to see me. Carmella and I laughed again at this.

After dinner, Cora asked for a sign. She wanted a sign like the psychic wanted. Something to clearly tell her this was truth—a phone call, perhaps, or a dream—she couldn't decide.

Carmella said, "Don't worry, God's plan will unfold." I was excited to see this happen. Moments later, Cora's phone rang. She didn't bother to check caller ID.

"Hello," said Cora.

"Hi, it's me, Ella." Ella and Cora had been friends for over thirty years. Ella totally believed in spirits and they had shared many conversations on the subject. Cora noticed that Ella sounded excited and a little nervous. "Oh, my God...I had to call you to tell you what happened today. I don't even know where to begin. I was reading the paper, the help-wanted ads, which you know I do every day. I came across this ad. You have to hear it." She began to read the job ad, and it sounded exactly like the description of what Ella had been looking for. She told Cora she called the company and asked for the woman named Vonnie, just as the ad read.

It turned out that Vonnie's name was misprinted in the ad and her real name was Connie. Connie explained that she had just taken over the company and was very interested to meet with Ella. They talked for over half-an-hour, and made plans to meet that afternoon.

"Cora, you are never going to believe this, but this is the same company that my grandmother predicted I'd be working at before she died; do you remember when she told me to apply a few months ago? And I did, but they told me they weren't hiring, so I never even got to fill out an application. Now I'm off to an interview. This is amazing!"

Ella's grandmother had recently died. Before her death, she had talked with Ella on many occasions about her job hunt. She told Ella that she was talented enough to work for that particular company and pushed her to apply. She said, "Ella, you never know, it can't hurt to apply. I think they will be so impressed, they'll hire you on the spot."

"It is a sign," Ella said. "The coincidences are too real. What is the chance that this company was sold to a lady named Connie, just like my grandmother's name, and that I now have an interview?!" Ella exclaimed.

The girls began to discuss the relevance of the sign. Cora felt it was a sign, too, but she was still skeptical. Carmella began to direct Cora's attention to a prayer she had on her refrigerator. It was the *Desiderata,* a poem by Max Ehrmann.

Go placidly amid the noise & haste, & remember what peace there may be in silence. As far as possible without surrender be on good terms with all persons.

Speak your truth quietly and clearly, and listen to others, even the dull and ignorant; they too have their story. Avoid loud and aggressive persons; they are the vexations to the spirit. Keep interested in your own career, however humble; it is a real possession in the changing fortunes of time. Exercise caution in your business affairs; for the world is full of trickery. But let this not blind you to what virtue there is; many persons strive for high ideals; and everywhere life is full of heroism.

Be Yourself.

Especially do not feign affection. Neither be cynical about love; for in the face of all aridity & disenchantment it is perennial as the grass. Take kindly the counsel of the years, gracefully surrending the things of youth.

Nurture strength of spirit to shield you in sudden misfortune. But do not distress yourself with imaginings. Many fears are born of fatigue & loneliness. Beyond a wholesome discipline, be gentle with yourself.

You are a child of the universe, no less than the trees & the stars; You have a right to be here. And whether or not it is clear to you, No doubt the universe is unfolding as it should.

Therefore be at peace with God, whatever you conceive Him to be, and whatever your labors & aspirations, in the noisy confusion of life, keep peace with your soul. With all its sham, drudgery & broken dreams, it is still a beautiful world. Be Cheerful. Strive to be Happy.

This was one of Carmella's favorite prayers. The prayer caught Cora's attention and she stopped talking and read it quietly. Ella heard the silence and asked, "Hello? Are you there? What's wrong?"

Cora replied, "Absolutely nothing." She paused and then said, "As we are questioning your sign, I have one right here. Listen to this…" And she read the prayer to her. They both agreed that prayer is what they should pursue—stop analyzing and go placidly amidst the noise and be happy. They agreed to be happy about the sign and Cora wished Ella good luck with the interview. "Go get that job!" Cora Said.

Cora reflected on this phone call and thought about the misspelling of the name. The letter "C" certainly could sound like the letter "V". A tiny bell went off in her head, I

126

don't need Ritalin, I need Rhealynn. She finally got the joke and smiled. She was a little crazy and apparently God sent her Rhealynn.

When Cora fell asleep that night, we came to her in a dream. During the dream, she woke up and wrote it down in as much detail as she could. Cora had kept a dream journal for years, and she often reread it for clarity. Tonight would be no exception. We gave her a glimpse of her future in hopes that she would see the light at the end of the tunnel.

She could not remember the details of her dream as she awoke feeling peaceful and rested. She mouthed the words, "Thank you" to us and climbed out of bed. Cora cheerfully got ready for work trying to remember the beautiful dream she had. She glanced over at her nightstand, saw her dream journal and quickly picked it up. The words she'd written the night before were almost illegible, as they often were when she jotted them down barely awake. She read her notes silently.

...nine months pregnant and in labor. I've arrived at the hospital and there are no doctors available. A midwife had come into my room. It is maybe 1920; I am having a boy. As the midwife says it's a boy, the baby cries, but soon the room grows quiet. The baby is dead. Its cord is tangled around its neck. (the writing got more illegible)... I'm walking in circles. I have woken up from this dream and written this. I awoke crying and screaming, my husband consoled me and reassured me it was only a dream, so I am going back to sleep.............

As Cora read these words, her memory was flooded with the dream's details. She became increasingly distraught. She was so glad that she had recorded the dream, but had mixed feelings about the dream itself. She needed to discuss her thoughts, so she called her godmother, Maria.

Maria was amazed at the dream because, as she explained to Cora, something similar actually happened to her own grandmother, Cora's great-grandmother.

Cora decided that she had to continue journaling each day. She laughed to herself that perhaps one day she'd write a book or even unlock the secret to life with her journal.

That night she wrote the following:

Today I learned that my great-grandmother carried
her first pregnancy to full term, yet once the baby
was delivered, he came out, cried and instantly died.
The cord had strangled him. This was 1921. In those
days, often a doctor was not present for the delivery
and so a midwife was. Midwives were not
experienced for these kinds of births. Had a doctor
been there, perhaps the baby would have lived.
I also learned that the baby was never buried. The
hospital took care of the body, however they did it
then. My great-grandmother wanted the baby
buried, but it wasn't the practice in those days.
When she learned she was pregnant the second
time, she went to Our Lady of Mount Carmel
Church and, during her seventh month, she walked
barefoot around the Carmelite statue? stature. She
prayed to St. Teresa and the Lady of Mt. Carmel.
She prayed for a healthy child. As she walked
around this statue, she vowed she would name this
baby after the lady if everything was okay. Her wish
was granted and Carmella was born.
I can't explain how I feel about this dream except
that it makes sense to me. Why? I understand that

my grandmother is communicating to me and now even through a dream...Dreams are usually about the past, but this feels like a warning for the future. Is this baby dream a gift from my grandmother about me having a baby? I hear you gram... "We know what you are going through, but we promise that your experience won't be so bad." I hear those words over and over...so it was her baby that died, not mine! It must be, that is how I need to feel. This has to be a beautiful dream, Grandma. You wouldn't tell me something bad would you? Oh what a beautiful dream, a dream of reassurance...yet what a horrible experience for my great-grandmother...I am so sorry for your loss. What was his name? ...Samuel..

We seem to have had a breakthrough; Cora can hear us better when she writes. As she journaled, she wrote our messages. Carmella talked with her granddaughter on paper for hours, answering all of her questions; however never telling her anything that wasn't allowed.

She was able to reassure her that her journey to motherhood was waiting. Even though there might be some bumps in the road, she would never have to go through what her great-grandmother had. The past was the past. Cora felt free as her pen flowed with her grandmother's words.

11
Life Existence

*When the potential for learning is exhausted, the
need to remain in the physical form in a particular
lifetime is considered complete.*
.~Rasha

Before I left my physical body, I had many
unanswered questions. Instead of praying to God for
understanding, I questioned why he was doing this to me and
my family. I knew I was returning to him, but selfishly, I
wanted more time—more time to have more experiences and
more time with my family.

Moments before my soul left my body, the answers
flowed thorough me like ocean waves. I knew who I was
created to be. I was destined to live for only a short time on
earth; I belonged to God. I had been given human
incarnation for the experience to remember what I was

created to be. The human mind unconsciously, yet consciously, chooses to forget that we choose incarnation for that experience.

It is free will which allows this choice to happen. Many souls journey through their human incarnation never remembering their true form; such was the case for me. I did consider myself an angel, but only because of the tasks I performed. Now I remember once again that I, Rhealynn, am a guardian angel.

I now remember that, as an angel, I was created by God to do good, as every spirit created by God is. Many angels have never had a human incarnation, however more and more of them exercise free will and choose to incarnate. I realize that this seems a little two-faced because I've explained that, as a human, you have free will, but as a spirit, you only have God's will. So it is hard for the human mind to understand that God's will embraces human incarnation. One day the ebb tide will caress you completely. Until then, many souls get tangled in their consciousness since their consciousness provides the exercise of free will and fear prevents acting with free will.

My journey has allowed me to remember that the conscious mind creates opinions and questions whenever the unconscious mind prompts them. The human experience develops confusion because, unconsciously, we know the answers that our conscious mind strives to understand. Many souls test for truth of the proof, so the conscious mind can understand.

Carmella's aura brightened as Cora's pen quickly scribbled our words. Even she knew this information would help her understand why she doubted herself. It wasn't that she lacked faith, but her conscious mind needed proof to trust what her soul understood as truth. Every time she began to understand why she doubted herself, she realized that acceptance was the lesson she needed most. She was often eager to communicate with us. Yet, when it happened, she questioned it and needed proof that it was real, instead of just accepting what it was.

She was finally beginning to understand that she need not fear us. Accepting that communication can happen with the afterlife, allowed her to remember that God's will was perfect.

As Cora was writing, she paused to remember what her friend Allison had said one day when she was feeling fearful of the words she was writing. Cora had told her, "I feel my pen flow and, as the words come into vision, I begin to read them and I get nervous. I wonder, is this truth or is this story? Sometimes, just as the story seems to be getting to a great part, I get too nervous to write. I want to read the story, but I cannot read it faster than I can write it down. I try to write faster, but I find that I cannot make the story unfold any faster than I can turn the hours on a clock."

Allison wisely replied, "Don't rush through writing because, if you go too fast, you might miss something important. You aren't suppose to turn the pages any faster because you need to cherish the moment you are in right now."

12
The Right Call, the Perfect Card & Carm

Waste no time talking about great souls and how they should be. Become one yourself!
~Marcus Aurelius

There are many days that Cora feels she could be losing her mind. After all, how sane was it to believe she could talk and clearly hear her grandmother and me, let alone all the other spirits and saints that she had communication with. She found herself in dire need of validation that this was all happening and she wished for clarity, but was still afraid of being spooked. All the information we shared with her was to prepare her for the future, not to scare her.

We gave her dreams to prepare her for the loss of a baby, so she could accept God's will. We gave her a few

137

visions regarding her friends and family, but, as she read many of these visions, she began to wonder if she was imagining or creating these stories.

She began to write everything down and, when she read what she wrote, her soul would echo the words, "Of course, that's it." The words on paper gave her clarity as her soul was being shaken into consciousness. The words were clear, but the message was scary. A miscarriage, an attack on a friend, a divorce—hopefully not her marriage, but whose? She wondered how she could change any of this knowledge she was getting. She was glad to have forewarning, but if she couldn't prevent anything, then why should she be told this information? No doubt her conscious mind questioned her sanity.

She knew she needed to find someone she trusted to talk with. She began to search anxiously through her phonebook for someone who might provide her with the strength to continue this journey or who could advise her that she certainly was on the wrong path. Her greatest fear was that she was being misled by her own consciousness. But she also felt compelled to continue because everything felt unbelievably true.

Her fingers quickly ran down each page of the phonebook, when Carmella forcefully stopped it at her family's priest, Father McCarthy. Carmella knew this would be the person Cora could talk with. However, Cora didn't know how to get in touch with him. She only had his address. Then something stunning happened. At the exact moment she was thinking this, her brother called.

He was calling to order flowers. As they talked, Cora casually asked, "Do you happen to have Father McCarthy's phone number?"

Her brother replied, "Yes, and thanks for reminding me that I have to call him myself. We've been playing phone tag regarding the wedding." Cora's brother was getting married in a few months and he wanted to ask Father McCarthy to perform the wedding ceremony. Cora got the number with a warning from her brother: "Father is very hard to get in touch with."

The phone then beeped and her brother had to quickly get the other call without ever asking why she needed the number.

The accessibility of getting Father McCarthy's number at that moment was a sure sign to Cora. She quietly thanked her grandmother. Cora stared at the number for a long time, rehearsing in her head what she would say. "Hi Father, I know we haven't talked in over a year, but I think I may be losing my mind. I can really hear and communicate with my dead grandmother and the signs I have been receiving are extremely intense and validating. I've had dreams that I found out were based on true lives; I've had visions of someone being murdered, another about someone getting divorced, another about someone getting accused of child abuse, and many many others. Am I just crazy or can I really be experiencing this?"

Cora could hear us laughing and knew we weren't laughing at her. We realized, however, that it all did sound a bit crazy. Cora knelt down and said a prayer with a request. "Dear God, whether or not I have some special gift of communication, I need to know. I need to know how to trust my own feelings. Please let Father guide me."

She dialed the number and remembered what her brother had said about Father being so hard to get in touch with. She knew if she didn't get to talk to him that night it wasn't meant to be.

His secretary answered the phone. "Hello, may I help you?"

Cora asked if she could speak with Father. The secretary said he was on another call and she could take a message.

Cora began to leave her number, when the phone beeped. The secretary asked if she could hold a minute while she answered the other line. Cora stayed on hold,

141

contemplating hanging up, when she heard Father's voice, "Hello, Cora, what's going on?"

Cora was almost speechless. She was talking directly to him, no phone tag, no message left; she barely had time to question the coincidence. Cora began to tell him quickly all that had been happening to her. She even told him how miraculous it was that he took her call that night. She was confident that God was with her, but she also needed reassurance that these things were true.

Father interrupted her by saying, "Isn't it beautiful." Cora was dumbstruck. It was true? Of course it was! She knew it! She continued telling him about all that she understood from our communications. She asked him, "Can people really talk with angels?"

He replied, "Of course."

She continued to ask him why God was communicating with her in this way, and told him of all the signs and her own thoughts of feeling crazy as she tried to understand everything.

Father interrupted her by saying, "Whoa, slow down. Cora, my dear, God is the epitome of simplicity. With all this analyzing, you are interpreting things to mean more that what God has intended."

He was right, Cora was very analytical. He chuckled as he said to her, "You sure are having a great ride; but, remember, all God wants is our unquestionable and unconditional love."

She understood this as he said it, yet felt bad that, as much faith as she had in God, she constantly did question Him to make sure she was on the right path and that everything was okay. She was always fearful that this communication was wrong. Talking with Father McCarthy was very helpful. Cora accepted that this was a great ride, she only wished for a sign to know that everything would be alright.

I reflected on the peace my mother received when she found my charm. I began to talk with my mom. She was reading a note that thanked her for recently shopping at

Cora's shop. It was a standard note sent out to new accounts, but Cora had handwritten a message saying, "It was a pleasure meeting you and, your daughter." Mom knew there was a connection between Cora and me, but she didn't know what it was.

Mom began writing a response note to Cora. As she did, she held my charm and realized what I was willing her to do.

> Dear Cora,
> It was a pleasure to meet you. I am sure that our meeting was pre-arranged. After I found this charm, I instantly thought of you and how I felt Rhealynn around you. I truly think that she would want you to have this charm, it meant so much to her. If it ever makes you feel uncomfortable, I would welcome it back, but I believe she wants it to be with you.
> God Bless.
> -Sandy (Rhealynn's mom)

Mom attached the prayer card from my funeral services, and the charm. She then researched Cora's home address and sent it. I was proud of her. Cora needed this sign. Everything was going to be okay.

13
Final Truths

*Dig within. Within is the wellspring of
Good; and it is always ready to bubble up, if you
just dig.*
.~Marcus Aurelius

The mail had already been delivered when Cora got home from work that day. She leafed through it and saw mostly bills. She stopped at a reminder card from her doctor's office. It reminded her that there was to be no eating or drinking prior to the surgery she'd scheduled for the following week to remove the damage to her uterus and ovary. She had recently found out that scar tissue and endometriosis was causing her infertility. Removal of this could improve the chances of her ability to conceive, however, she would also need months of chemical therapy to attempt to rebuild the damage. The doctors were hopeful that she would be able to carry a child full term.

Cora was startled by the sound of someone adjusting her screen door. She looked up and noticed that the mailman was walking away.

He looked back when he heard the door open. "Sorry to disturb you, I left a letter in the doorway," he said, as he looked to the ground where it had fallen after Cora had opened the door. "I should have rung the bell."

"No worries," Cora said, as she attempted to pick up the letter. She laughed when a gust of wind blew it down two steps Once she caught up to the letter, she grabbed it and yelled "thanks" to the mailman.

The handwriting wasn't familiar and there was no return address on the envelope. She walked into her kitchen and opened the letter. The charm promptly fell out and Cora felt chills run through her as she heard me say that the angel charm was mine. She read the note and stood in awe of, not only its message, but the generosity of my mother to part with the charm.

She spoke to me and said, "Rhealynn, I get it. Everything is alright with me; but if I have this charm does that mean things aren't alright with your mother?"

I told her that I wanted her to have, not only this message, but to hold something in her hand that I held so close to my heart. I told her, "If it makes you feel uncomfortable, you can return it to my mom."

She expressed her thankfulness. In the meantime, the rest of the unopened mail was still on the counter. She glanced at it and realized that, behind the flyers was a purple envelope. It was obvious that it was a card. The corner of the envelope had her godfather's return address. "How appropriate," she said to me. "How could I not have seen this card before? I suppose because you wanted me to open it at the right time." She smiled as she held the charm in the palm of her hand and opened the purple envelope. The card had a photograph of a young girl, around the age of five, standing in the middle of a parking lot on a beautiful day, holding an umbrella while rain sprinkled all around her. Cora embraced the beauty and was eager to read the caption inside. Her eyes began to well as she read the words printed. It read; "The secret to life is anticipating the rainbows."

Cora began to glow. She knew this card and my charm were proof that everything was going to be okay. The card reminded her of the rain story that her mother told her. The rain story was so beautiful she thought. This really is the meaning of life.

While she was still embracing those thoughts, her phone rang. This time it was her girlfriend Tia. Tia had been friends with Cora since sixth grade. She didn't really believe in all this psychic stuff; it spooked her and made her think that Cora was, perhaps, going over the edge. Tia had been skeptical of all Cora had been going through. Yet, Cora didn't hold back on the phone. She told Tia about the day's events. Tia thought about it and said, "Well, I suppose everything happens for a reason."

"Well, then," replied Cora, "you must have a part to play. What is the reason for your call, have you unlocked the mystery of all this yet?"

Tia replied that she really had no idea, but she told Cora that she had been thinking about the story of the rainbow. "Cora, what if the rain that your mother talked about did baptize and cleanse all the souls that needed it, then wouldn't the rainbow be the bridge to heaven?"

Cora shook with delight at the thought. "It could be, Tia. Just think about how the earth must feel after a good rainstorm. Refreshed, cleansed, and thirst-quenched. Everyone anticipates a rainbow after the rain goes. We pause to admire it and often we share that we saw the rainbow. Our soul knows the real meaning of a rainstorm. That is why our mind anticipates a rainbow."

And that was it. Our journeys are a rainstorm and, with each tomorrow, more rain will come, so anticipate the rainbow's message now.

Surgery day arrived. Cora was putting her shoes on and glanced at the clock. The time was 11:11, a time when wishes are granted. She prayed that the surgery would help her journey to motherhood, as well as continue her journey toward the rainbow. She thanked God, all the angels, the saints, and us.

Johanna drove her to the hospital that day. Once in the car, Cora looked at the console and noticed what appeared to be a snack bar full of prayer cards. She heard a voice say, "My child you have asked and you shall receive."

When Johanna saw her looking at the cards, she said, "I brought them to pray while you are in surgery."

"No, Mom. I'll be fine; don't worry."

Her mother said, "I know you will, but I still want to take them; well, I'll take one." She reached for the top card and took the one under it. It was St. Theresa.

Cora's husband met her at the hospital. As she was wheeled into the surgical suite, he held her hand. He smiled down on her saying, "I love you; everything will be fine. Go to sleep. It will be all be over in a few minutes, and I will be right here."

As she drifted off to sleep, Carmella and I held her hands, whispering to her that everything would be okay. We were so proud of her.

14
The Beginning

Carl Jung called it "Synchronicity". We call it coincidence. Serendipity. Luck. Chance. Fate. We call it everything but what it really is: Grace. God.
~Sarah Ban Breathnach

Many people would not want to know what lies ahead, but the journey to wisdom can be inspiring for those who do. The answers to life are so simple, but to understand them as a human is very complex. When we guide you, we want to tell you the truth, which your soul not only yearns for but already knows. The problem, as you have seen, is that when the soul is in the physical body, it gets distracted from the truth.

If you stub your toe and it turns green, you might ask, why. The simple answer might be that you stubbed your toe. But the journey through the why, can take you places you never imagined. The answers in life are simple, but exploring the questions is the complexity of the journey.

Many souls journey to the answer and others journey for the lesson. Some lessons are meant to be taught and some lessons are asked to be learned. You have free will to chose; do you want to see the truths in black or white, or in color? There is no wrong answer to that question.

Cora will continue her journey, often questioning the answers she receives. These questions allow lessons to paint pictures for her conscious mind. Then she can understand the wisdom her soul knows. The road to discovery is found along the rainbow, below, above, on, and in it. The discovery is the acceptance and knowledge of your soul's merge with the rainbow. The journey is worth everything. Do not have fear of learning, exploring, understanding, and accepting because, in the end, you will know. Everything is okay.

> *Dear Mom,*
> *I love you; I am holding your hand, but you can*
> *hear me no more. I have to go now, please don't be*

sad. You gave me life to experience all I need so that my journey may continue.

Oh Lord, I see you in the glorious light, coming for me. I am torn, fighting to hold my mother's hand a little longer, but I hear my name being called and I want to return. I remember this voice; Mom can you hear it? It is beautiful, I am so excited, I wish you could know how excited I am. Please let me go; we will be together soon. I will watch over you always. You love me, I know. I know this love, it is encompassing me, carrying into this heavenly light. Here I come, here I come.....

I am back.

With songs of thanksgiving, a shower of warm colors welcome me as I cross the bridge...I am speechless except for thank you, thank you for this trip. It is truly wonderful.

I want to ask the whys, to find the answers; but, I see it instantly. Oh!...it's magnificent! What a picture! Where I am..I am still needed...........................this is going to be so beautiful!

Love,

Rhealynn

I can write no more. I have seen things which make all that I have written seem like straw."

~Saint Thomas Aquinas

Desiderata
By Max Ehrmann

Go placidly amid the noise & haste, & remember what peace there may be in silence. As far as possible without surrender be on good terms with all persons. Speak your truth quietly and clearly, and listen to others, even the dull and ignorant; they too have their story.

Avoid loud and aggressive persons; they are the vexations to the spirit. Keep interested in your own career, however humble; it is a real possession in the changing fortunes of time.

Exercise caution in your business affairs; for the world is full of trickery. But let this not blind you to what virtue there is; many persons strive for high ideals; and everywhere life is full of heroism.

Be Yourself.

Especially do not feign affection. Neither be cynical about love; for in the face of all aridity & disenchantment it is perennial as the grass.

Take kindly the counsel of the years, gracefully surrending the things of youth. Nurture strength of spirit to shield you in sudden misfortune. But do not distress yourself with imaginings. Many fears are born of fatigue & loneliness. Beyond a wholesome discipline, be gentle with yourself.

You are a child of the universe, no less than the trees & the stars; You have a right to be here. And whether or not it is clear to you, No doubt the universe is unfolding as it should.

Therefore be at peace with God, whatever you conceive Him to be, and whatever your labors & aspirations, in the noisy confusion of life, keep peace with your soul. With all its sham, drudgery & broken dreams, it is still a beautiful world.

Be Cheerful.   Strive to be Happy.

A Note from the Author

*This story was written in 1999; I assume at least another three
years would pass before this book, if ever, was ever published.
My dear friend, Kay, told me there was no hurry to finish it,
even though I felt a calling to. I often reread it, seldom edited it,
and always wanted to write more, but wasn't moved. I have
written several other stories, but I never could rewrite this one.*

*Over the years, I have had many "God moments" and angelic
experiences. I often write them in hopes of having a collection
of short stories that, perhaps, one day I will be comfortable to
share. The angel in this story represents God's love; and I have
witnessed on many occasions that unconditional healing love. I
have seen a friend be cured of cancer, and again survive a
brutal attack. I have seen miracles of organ transplants, cancer
remissions, and countless acts of God's mercy to families that
have lost loved ones tragically. I have felt my grandfather
peacefully leave this earth on the wing of an angel, and, most
importantly, I have been given the gift of carrying life.*

*As a mother of two beautiful daughters, I am thankful to God
for his unconditional love, patience and forgiveness. I know it
is because of His love that writing this story could give me
clarity and comfort. I will share with you that I did have a
miscarriage and it was hard, but the journey to motherhood has
been worth every moment, just as the journey of life is worth
every story.*

*My hope is that, by sharing this story, you may be embraced in
God's love. God loves you. He will never leave you, nor do your
loved ones. And if you doubt, know there is always hope.*

Special Thanks to my husband; thanks for giving me the encouragement to continue writing. I appreciate your patience, your guidance, and your acceptance of my opinions. I trust you with all my heart. Thank you for your love and support always.

To my precious daughters, my heaven sent angels, who know my soul like no other, as they journeyed through my soul and with my soul forever. Thank you for all your sweet hugs and your unconditional gift of love. I also want to thank my entire family; especially my brothers, my godmother; and most importantly my parents, who first taught me unconditional love. I thank you all for providing me with a safety net whenever I felt I was falling.

To my friends, my support team, Kay, Andrea, Katie, Rachael, Kristen, Danielle, Charlene, & Sarah, who loan their professional talents to my shop, making it a special place. I thank them for their tireless support. Especially Danielle and Kay, who many nights took my phone calls and provided me with the encouragement to continue this journey.

Thanks to Father George Farland of Sacred Heart Church in Springfield, MA. Your ears heard me when I was most in need of church support. Also, to Father Jerry McGrath of St. Anthony's Cathedral in Galveston, Texas; thank you for taking my call and reminding me that God is simple. You truly encourage me to "enjoy the ride".

There are so many others I wish to thank, including all my cousins, and my friends. I appreciate you all for accepting me and allowing me to be me. Thanks to Kristie, Shelley & Ava, for sharing in the journey. Special thanks to Kim Dotiwalla, Tricia O'Grady-Howard, Annah Simone, Karin Kane, Karen Fletcher, Steven Marcus, Korby Clark, Pam Tully, Sarah Gale, Members of the Blair family; and my daughter Maggie for their helping to edit my grammar, and encouraging me to continue on this writing journey.

To St. Theresa, my special confident, who knows me as herself and continues to teach me her ways. To Mary, thank you for watching over my words so carefully.

Finally, I wish to remember with thanks all the angels that guided me to write this story. My grandmother, Mildred Shuman; my dear friend, Timmy Sunstrom; and my new friend, Andrea Borsari, who I may have never met on earth, but I know that I have met on the rainbow that links heaven to earth. In her memory, I dedicate this book to God, whose unconditional love constantly grabs my attention. Thank you.

Made in the USA
Middletown, DE
15 April 2015